- Develop Entrepreneurial Attributes
- Create and Grow the New Venture
- Minimize Capital Needs
- Make Bad Guys Finish Last

THE EFFECTIVE ENTREPRENEUR

AND HOW TO MAKE BAD GUYS FINISH LAST

Gardner H. Russell

ADVANTAGE PUBLISHING
P.O. Box 372358
Satellite Beach, Florida 32937
407-777-4548 407-773-7085 Fax

Copyright © 1999 Gardner H. Russell

Published by Advantage Publishing,
P.O. Box 372358, Satellite Beach, Florida, 32937.
Printed in the United States of America

Library of Congress Catalogue Card Number 98-96688

Russell, Gardner
    The effective entrepreneur/and how to make bad guys
        finish last./by Gardner H. Russell

ISBN Number 0-9668238-0-X   SAN 299 7436
1. New business enterprises--United States. 2. Entrepreneurship--United States. 3. Self-employed--United States. 4. Small business-United States. 1. Title.

PREFACE

The author has achieved broad, rarely-equalled, hands-on experience in entrepreneurship. By acquiring, creating, growing, and capitalizing more than a half-dozen manufacturing and other business entities, he exceeded the entrepreneurial norm of "5 projects by age 55".

A graduate of Miami University, Oxford, Ohio, he served in a "cloak and dagger" capacity for the U.S. Army, G-2, M.I.S. during World War II as Executive for Intelligence to the Military Attaches in our Embassies of Argentina, Brazil, Costa Rica, and Mexico.

His first business experience was in San Francisco, California, in export and domestic sales. There followed entrepreneurial ventures: leveraged buyouts of floundering manufacturing companies, consulting services to dozens of others.

In recent years Mr. Russell was called by the First Presidency of the Church of Jesus Christ of Latter-day Saints, to serve full-time in Mexico and Central America in the Quorums of the Seventy, as one of the General Authorities.

He continues to provide consulting services to business, and serves as advisor to various Boards of Directors and Boards of Trustees.

Warm weather and water lovers, the author and his wife Dorothy reside on a barrier reef in Satellite Beach, Florida, on the Main Canal which accesses the Banana River and Inland Waterway. It is a short trip by boat to their youngest daughter's as well as to their son's home. Another daughter lives on the mainland, where the Russell clan gathers when hurricanes threaten. Their oldest daughter lives in Manhattan. They enjoy their 14 grandchildren.

INTRODUCTION

THE EFFECTIVE ENTREPRENEUR is dedicated to tens of thousands of entrepreneurs who are already embarked upon their new ventures; to thousands more who have made the *Big Decision* and are actively planning that first business; and to countless *"wannabes"*, *Good Guys* , men and women who yearn to be in their own enterprises.

Actual case studies, *"Illustration Capsules"*, are interspersed in the narrative for clarity, and *"Premises"*, suggestions and recommendations, are italicized for ready reference.

Good Guys, and, especially, Good *Guys with Bad Luck,* whomsoever and wherever they may be, will learn how to become more *effective entrepreneurs*, and ways to protect themselves against *Bad Guys*.

A *Bad Guy* is defined for our purposes as "Anyone who, by any means, seeks to take away the assets of *Good Guys."*

The author is indebted to hundreds of *Bad Guys*, many of whom he has made Finish Last, and whose methods he has carefully observed, studied, analyzed and experienced over several decades, as they assiduously set about to attack and divest the *Good Guys* of their assets.

May the reader, one of the *Good Guys*, learn and apply the lessons of this volume to succeed in becoming an *Effective Entrepreneur* , and making *Bad Guys Finish Last.*

Good luck!

To my wife Dorothy Annette Russell and mentors
U.S. Congressman Burton Lee French and Dr. Harry
J. Russell, Ph.D., father, example, and author.

TABLE OF CONTENTS

CHAPTER ONE

THE WOULD-BE ENTREPRENEUR

T ens of thousands of individuals are entrepreneurial 'wannabes' who are *constrained by obvious realities:* (1) a built-in fear of change, (2) the perceived security of a regular paycheck, and (3) the *corporate promise* of job security and retirement. Their latent entrepreneurial spirit is anesthesized. If you are a *would-be entrepreneur,* you *will* find in this book proven ways to embark on your own success-ful entrepreneurial venture. And, if you are already struggling with that new business, you will find valuable methods to increase your assets and protect them from the Bad Guys.

Internal and External Entrepreneurs

Internal Voluntary Entrepreneurs are employees of pri-vate and public corporations and other institutions, who feel the need to develop entrepreneurial attributes for the benefit of their employer. Until recently this was either discouraged by Corporate America, ignored, or given lip service. In recent years, enlightened employers have discovered that encourag-ing and nurturing quiescent entrepreneurship in select em-ployees will result in measurable value-added benefits, in addition to better morale and less turnover.

There are a few companies specializing in seminars and

one-on-one training, and books on the subject authored by well-known business writers. There is a curriculum in a number of universities, designed to develop necessary entrepreneurial attributes in corporate employees.

External Voluntary Entrepreneurs are individuals who plan early in their careers to create a new venture or acquire an existing one. They typically work for a period in corporate or institutional entities until they have gained enough experience and seed capital to organize the new enterprise. This experience is important. There are those who believe a good idea and financial resources are sufficient to begin the business without such experience. There is a high failure rate in such 'PFTA' (plucked-from-thin-air) start-ups. Those who do succeed often pay a heavy price for their trial-and-error, on-the-job training.

The Corporate Promise and the Involuntary Entrepreneur

Involuntary Entrepreneurs are men and women forced into entrepreneurial activity due to termination by the employer, or the realization that they are either unable or unwilling to continue to work for others. They number in the thousands. Corporations, private and public, are the greatest source of involuntary entrepreneurs. As noted, the breakdown of the traditional corporate promise of job retention and pension has forced many to take the entrepreneurial plunge.

Many factors, not the least of which is the increasingly complex global economy and proliferation of multinational companies, have adversely affected the corporate promise. Once sacrosanct company pension plans are now on the endangered species list and post-retirement health care commitments are diminished or disavowed. There are more broken or missing rungs on the corporate ladder than ever before. Downsizing, re-engineering and rightsizing -- all euphemisms for termination -- continue unabated. Layoff bloodletting is a fact of life. Few companies are untouched. Fear of losing one's job in many areas is endemic.

That the unspoken corporate promise is no longer a reality is starkly apparent as employees in many areas, once terminated, are unable to find acceptable employment. Many find themselves thrust involuntarily into the marketplace, resulting in shotgun entrepreneurial marriages. Near-caesarean births of thousands of these new businesses have created tens of thousands of new jobs and a sharp upsurge in the strength of the marketplace.

The Corporate Game

Most company policy-makers believe that key executives, once they acquire sufficient capital, will leave to organize their own ventures. Enter the *corporate game*. The executive is informed that with each promotion, he or she will be *expected* to live on a scale befitting the position, to purchase a larger home in an upscale neighborhood, to entertain, to join an exclusive country club, to take expensive vacations, to place children in private schools, etc.

Expenses rise inexorably to match or surpass income. Asset formation, equity growth, and cash position are minimal. And today's executive is especially vulnerable to attrition in middle and top management positions resulting from mergers, acquisitions, or spin-offs. While the more fortunate are able to fund new ventures by golden handshakes and favorable asset bases, the majority are not so lucky. Not only do they have few assets, they are burdened with heavy debt, locked in to high standards of living by their former positions.

The Voluntary Entrepreneur

More and more corporate employees view their present employment as a stepping stone to entrepreneurship, following a preconceived plan. As soon as they acquire the ingredients of experience, seed capital, etc., they resign to organize the new venture. Should corporate downsizing, acquisitions, or mergers terminate their employment before the planned departure date, they launch their preemie first venture with minimal anxiety, since their plan is largely in place.

There are two main types of *voluntary entrepreneurs*: First are the corporate employees described previously who consciously prepare for their departure. These individuals will remain employed only until they acquire the necessary experience, know-how and capital to depart. Second are the individuals who find they are not well suited to the corporate environment for personality, political or other reasons.

Whether entrepreneurs be voluntary or involuntary, they share the same strong commitment to their new enterprises and, in an overwhelming number of cases, their spouses are supportive (although they may prefer a steady paycheck).

Entrepreneurs Are Made -- Not Born

It was once believed that entrepreneurs were born -- not made. While is true that there are those who seem destined from birth to innovate and create, it has become obvious that many men and women *can and do learn* to be entrepreneurs. It is probable that the reader already enjoys basic entrepreneurial traits which can be improved and refined. Other attributes can usually be learned. While there are certain basic concepts to guide the new entrepreneur, the 'trial-and-error' method is *not* the route to take.

It is advisable to first obtain sufficient business knowledge and experience by working for others. Secondly, one needs to acquire -- preferably by saving and careful investment -- an adequate amount of seed capital for the first new venture. A business plan with profit-and-loss and cash flow projections is a must. Some product market verification is also desirable (contrary to sales lore, Eskimos do not usually purchase freezers for their igloos). *Analysis-to-paralysis* is not our goal, but sufficient understanding of the marketplace, the product or service and its potential is very important. And, not the least consideration is that the new venture should be personally exciting, challenging and fun.

Entrepreneur Defined

There are seemingly as many definitions of *Entrepreneur* and *Entrepreneurship* as there are writers who treat the subject. As the 21st Century arrives, new and expanded definitions of entrepreneurs and entrepreneurship will undoubtedly come forth. Ten years ago, few had logged on to the Internet. Now, new fortunes are being made every day by entrepreneurs creative and bold enough to exploit this technology.

Earliest Origins

The word entrepreneur is of French origin. As early as the 15th century, a Frenchman named Cantillon may have been the first to invent the word 'entrepreneur' and define it as, *"The agent who purchases the means of production for combination into marketable products."*

Three hundred years after Cantillon, another of his countrymen recorded a further definition. J. B. Say described the entrepreneur of his day as, *"The organizer of a business firm central to its distributive and production functions."* These definitions describe primarily economic functions.

Contemporary Definitions

One of the deans of modern entrepreneurial knowledge and study is Joseph R. Mancuso of the Center for Entrepreneurial Studies and Management, Inc. He provides this insightful description:

"Essentially, entrepreneurs are innovators, combining different technologies or business concepts to produce marketable products or services. They fill-in the people, financing, production, and marketing gaps by acquiring and assembling the necessary resources into newly created firms. But, foremost they are able to recognize potentially profitable opportunities to conceptualize the venture strategy, and to become the key force in successfully moving their ideas from the laboratory to the marketplace. Those who 'go it alone' are usually the firstborn in families having a self-employed parent, whose successes result in the

entrepreneur's high need for achievement. Often formal education is pursued to the extent that a master's degree is obtained."

In *SUCCESS Magazine* we read, "You can't build a single psychological profile of the entrepreneur. There are too many examples that break the rules." (April 1993). Perhaps, but there *are* ways to evaluate the management personality and style to identify entrepreneurial attributes.

The Entrepreneurial Spirit

Scientists estimate that 3 million years ago, precursors of modern man had brains weighing one pound. After 2 million years the brain weight more than doubled. During those millennia, fossilized remains indicate that prehistoric man represented a delicacy to predators like the saber-toothed tiger. Our ancestors survived by hiding in caves or in the primeval forest, nearly defenseless. Then someone fashioned a sharp tool, chipped laboriously from flint, to perhaps scrape animal skins. He may have been carrying this handy tool when attacked by a tiger. In desperation, he may have used the sharp implement to attempt to defend himself, which caused the tiger to rethink its intended prey. Later, while nursing claw wounds, the caveman may have affixed the point to a shaft and wrapped it with a tough vine -- and the spear was born. The playing field was levelled, and man became the hunter instead of the hunted. Archeological finds of gnawed tiger bones attest to his entrepreneurial genius, and as proof, we note that his descendants outlived the saber-toothed tiger.

Though the above story is anecdotal, man's entrepreneurial activity was, from the beginning, essential to survival. Nearly all religions and traditions bespeak of some sort of a Creation. In the Judeo-Christian faiths, Adam and Eve were unquestionably the first entrepreneurs with their celestial training. The Book of Genesis records that Adam received instruction from Jehovah about how to till the earth. Whatever our belief, it cannot be disputed that we are recipients, to a greater or lesser degree, of imprint and perhaps even entrepreneurial genes from the very beginnings of our race. Many centuries later, our more recent ancestors, the pilgrims and pioneers, were imbued with a driving entrepreneurial spirit.

The concept that the entrepreneurial spirit is somehow *imprinted* in us is strengthened today by studies finding that if members of one's family have been entrepreneurial, the same spirit is often nurtured in an offspring. Thus a son or daughter, grandson or granddaughter, more often than not, becomes an active entrepreneur. In some families the spirit may lie dormant for years, sometimes even for generations, only to burst into flower in a successful entrepreneur.

So, both theses -- that entrepreneurs are either 'born' or 'made' -- are correct. There can be little doubt, however, that slavery, indentured servitude, desperate poverty, and centuries of oppression have stifled and continue to sublimate that spirit of innovation and creation in millions of people. And in more recent times, corporate life with its perceived security; the professions; the trades, all have -- by their structured and restrictive nature -- played and continue to play a part in recessing the entrepreneurial spirit (or genes) to but a tiny blip on the screen of many people's lives.

Behind the Successful Entrepreneur

It has been said that a successful entrepreneur is the product of one or more failures. And it is also said, albeit facetiously, that behind the successful entrepreneur (most are married) is a mother--in-law who cannot believe it and possibly never will, and a spouse who still misses the regular paycheck.

Entrepreneurial experience can be acquired and vital attributes learned. In the next pages are keys to prepare for, then embark on that *new venture,* and hopefully, enjoy the success and rewards -- both financial and personal -- that entrepreneurship offers. However, if the first venture is a failure or runs into serious trouble, there are proven ways to keep assets intact and *Make Bad Guys Finish Last* so one can begin again.

Common Traits and Attributes

Some traits and attributes common to the entrepreneur are:
- intense curiosity
- an unwillingness or inability to work in structured public or private activity
- an avid reader of books and magazines
- an accomplished networker in an endless quest for knowledge in many areas
- an ability to identify and combine known technologies to create a new product or service
- a feel for the market niche of a new product
- a drive to succeed and willingness to work
- business activities as a youth

- need for independence
- ability to make good decisions
- distills the essential from a mass of data
- quite personable
- a people-person
- high self-esteem and self-confidence
- achievement, not money, driven
- views possible failure(s) as a learning process toward eventual success
- there are no problems, only challenges
- rerum novarum cupidus (is driven to new things)
- computer literate in word processing, spreadsheets

Although experts differ on what constitutes an entrepreneur, they do agree that the basic attributes critical to entrepreneurship can be learned. It is now recognized that even a person working in a so-called 'trustee' or 'refining' capacity typical of management in large private or public companies might blossom (if given the opportunity) into successful activity as an *internal entrepreneur*. Such individual contributions can be of significant value once these skills are recognized and encouraged by the organization.

Our emphasis will be upon the *external entrepreneur* -- the person who independently develops products or services which answer a specific and unattended need in the marketplace, usually in a definite and measurable niche. We will not dwell on either the meteoric rise of those few who have ascended to Fortune 500 or 1000 status, large private and public corporations controlled by entrepreneurs, or multi-millionaires whose success is so well-chronicled by the media. Nor will we treat further the aspects of internal entrepreneurs performing within large companies.

The Sole Proprietor

Though the sole proprietor is vital to our communities and their economic fabric, he or she may not necessarily be entrepreneurial. The requirements, traits and attributes of the owner of an existing business are less demanding than those required for most entrepreneurial start-ups. Basic management skills are usually sufficient. A majority of these "Mom and Pop" stores, have known and measured parameters. They focus on the available customer base and are usually retail in nature. Little new value is added.

An entrepreneur might view retail product or service outlets as stifling and restrictive -- that waiting at a location all day for customers to arrive, busying oneself with records, inventory, point-of-sale displays, shrinkage and obsolescence, and working endlessly on record-keeping -- is somehow akin to the spider that spins its web in a likely place and waits for its victims. In the retail outlet, the owner 'tends the web, rearranges and renews filaments and waits.' This scenario of waiting is the antithesis of the creative entrepreneur who is driven to innovate, reach out and create new value.

Entrepreneurs In Transition

Having said this, there are sole proprietors who become outstanding entrepreneurs by exploiting new niches. For example, when the sole owner of a store or service business identifies a niche for expansion of products or services or develops the business into a franchise operation or a chain of stores, a new entrepreneur is born and new value created.

Examples abound of former sole proprietors who are

entrepreneurs in transition. Like the ice cream maker who began with one store and now owns huge manufacturing plants servicing thousands of outlets. Or the housewife/cookie-maker who first opened one store and now has hundreds of franchised and company-owned stores. Or J. Willard Marriott, who started a 'Hot Shoppe' and became owner and franchiser of hotels. And the man who borrowed from his in-laws to buy the first grocery store, invented the nesting grocery cart and created an empire of supermarkets, shopping centers, and more. *Premise: Entrepreneurs can rarely be happy in sole proprietorships, but sole proprietors can and do become successful entrepreneurs.*

The Inventor-Entrepreneur

One of our national characteristics is that nearly every adult has (1) at least one idea for a business (usually not viable), and (2) an opinion, well-informed or not (usually not), about almost any subject. Many years ago, while employed as Export Manager of Soulé Steel Company in San Francisco, I listened incredulously as, day after day, a garrulous elevator operator assailed his captive audiences with a barrage of uninformed opinions. My reactions varied from irritation to indignation, while others merely ignored or endured. Though I had not yet learned that I was not suited to the corporate environment, I was being primed as an entrepreneur.

In my mind, I had already made the decision to change my career path from export or domestic sales to manufacturing. So, when an offer came to save a start-up manufacturing company in Puerto Rico, I eagerly accepted. The Bay Area 'know-it-alls' and the garrulous elevator operator were just added reasons to accept the offer as Plant Manager of a jalousie manufacturing company. In the Island of Enchantment, thankfully, few people gratuitously expressed an opinion, and rarely did anyone regale me with ideas about a new product or service. There followed more than 20 years of successful, challenging and often exhilarating experiences as a manufacturer, consultant and inventor-entrepreneur under the Federal income tax-free *Operation Bootstrap* of the Government of Puerto Rico.

The Better Mousetrap

A word about inventors, inventor-entrepreneurs and would-be inventors. As for the latter, it is rare to find a man or woman, old or young, who does not have a 'great idea' for some kind of an invention. The unfortunate reality is that at least 90 percent of these concepts do not bear up under scrutiny, usually because the product is not viable and/or there is little or no market of substance.

The old maxim was:

*"Build a better mousetrap and the world will beat a path to your door."** *

The new premise is:

"Nearly anything that can be sold can be made."

This is largely true. New products automatically become irrelevant in the absence of a pretested market niche.

---

* The exact quote from Ralph Waldo Emerson, *"If a man write a better book, preach a better sermon, or make a better mousetrap than his neighbor, tho' he build his house in the woods, the world will make a beaten path to his door."*

There will probably never be a 'better mousetrap' because it could not compete with the traditional wood-mounted trigger-bail device.

A possible exception might be the invention of a multiple entry trap that would instantaneously vaporize the rodent in some fashion. The fastidious or squeamish would buy such a trap because cost would be no object. But, this would probably account for only a thin slice of the available market.

My farmer-uncle in Jensen, Utah, once showed me how to make a do-it-yourself mousetrap. He inserted a stiff wire through the eyelets holding the bail of a milk pail, partly-filled it with water, and squeezed a lump of dough around the wire at its midpoint. Mice easily maintained their balance along the wire, crawled onto the dough which, providing no claw-hold, promptly rotated and dropped the mouse into the water below.

But even my uncle reverted to the baited 'click-snap' wood-mounted trigger-bail trap.

New innovations have not created a better mousetrap. But, a different technology has taken over. A few traps cling forlornly to a corner of the store shelf, which is now filled with a variety of poison baits. No matter that the rodent will die in the wall and make its 'presence known' for days or weeks.

Would-Be Inventor-Entrepreneurs

Most of us know of one or more would-be inventors who, convinced of the value of their creation, doggedly continue to refine and perfect their inventions over months and years. They live off savings, loans from family, banks and others -- doomed to failure in the absence of a viable market for their product or service.

There is also a small group of inventors which rarely start a new business, because they can never quite bring forth a production prototype. They constantly strive to improve the product -- continuing to tinker, create and recreate -- long after the item is ready for the market. Like the would-be inventor, they are possessive and reflect a dog-in-the-manger attitude.

They can't do what is required to transform the invention into a viable business. Yet, they will not let anyone else provide the services needed.

There are the hundreds of dedicated and sometimes inspired inventors who envision, create and bring a series of successful products to market. Some are *pure inventor-entrepreneurs*, content to develop production prototypes, license the technology to a manufacturer, and receive license fees and royalties on sales of the product, then move on to new challenging inventing opportunities.

In a class by themselves, are the *inventor-entrepreneurs* who also share a devotion to their invention, yet their true desire is to devote all necessary assets, time and efforts to bring it to market. They often manufacture prototypes in their garages or modest rental spaces. When a production prototype is debugged and field tested, they set up a small shop to manufacture the final product, and market the product themselves. They fervently try to retain 100 percent of the equity interest. However, in their desire to see the new enterprise succeed, they become targets for unscrupulous investors.

The "Bump-and-Run"

It's not uncommon for an inventor-entrepreneur to be initially successful. Example: Let's suppose that the owner generates $100,000 from savings, mortgages, family, friends, etc., and begins production. Sales reach $300,000 the first year of operations. Gross profit is a high percentage of net sales. There is a 12 percent net profit after taxes, or $36,000. Second year sales triple to $1 million with $150,000, or 15 percent of sales net profit after taxes. Future prospects are excellent.

But suddenly and -- to the owner -- unexpectedly, positive cash flow falters. It is a challenge to meet payables, withholding and social security taxes, and other business obligations. The entrepreneur is confused, not realizing that the business has become *too successful.* He or she is unaware of the unforgiving business rule-of-thumb that says that, as a minimum, 15 percent of net annual sales will be required in working capital just to service accounts receivable. And, the two months inventory of materials and factory supplies, 25 percent of sales in the case of the new company (let's call it Newco), require additional operating funds. This does not include outlays for the acquisition of new machinery, equipment maintenance, research and development, etc.

Let us suppose that $10,000 cash remains from the initial paid-in capital of $100,000. Thus the total available working capital from the initial investment, plus earnings and current profits *after taxes* at the beginning of the third year, is $196,000 ($10,000 cash remaining from paid-in capital plus $36,000 first year earnings, plus $150,000 second year profits).

Sales are projected at $1,500,000 for the third year of operations, which will require additional General and Administrative expenses. There is, therefore, a shortfall (or negative cash flow) at the end of the second year of about $100,000.

To cover this negative cash flow situation, the inventor-entrepreneur visits a banker with profit-and-loss and cash flow projection spreadsheets in hand, or -- more often than not -- with only an independent accountant's 2-year Operating and Financial Statements. Business prospects are bright. But the bank is not interested in providing a loan, due to insufficient collateral.

The entrepreneur is forced to seek investors. Obsessed with retaining control of the company, he or she is unable to attract substantial funds. Nights are sleepless, the business precarious.

Enter the "Bump-and-Run" investor, who calms and reassures the inventor-entrepreneur; offers to invest whatever amounts of capital are needed, taking only a minority interest. Both parties agree that, since the company is only 2 years old, the market value of the business is three times (instead of perhaps five times or more) the average annual earnings before taxes. The value of the company is set at $1 million at the insistence of the owner.

The investor says, "We are willing to back you and invest whatever your company needs. Our stock interest will be pro-rata based on the value which you set on the company. Please ask for all you will need, because if you come to us later for additional funds, it will be a *different conversation*."

The owner doesn't hear, or at least pays no attention, to the warning. He is preoccupied with the desire to limit the amount of outside ownership, and to prove to the investor that he can manage the business with the least possible additional capital. Even though projections indicate a minimum of $400,000 will be needed, the inventor-entrepreneur believes $300,000 will suffice.

"All right, Mr. Investor, according to the agreed formula, for an investment of $300,000, I will sell you a 30 percent common voting stock interest in the Company."

"Good. You have our commitment to invest $300,000 for 30 percent of the common voting stock of the company. Now, are you *sure* this is enough for your ongoing capital needs?"

The answer is in the affirmative.

"Remember, it is important that you understand that if you need more investment later on, there will be a different conversation. If you need more capital now, just say so." The investor has put the entrepreneur on notice. The "Bump" is completed. With the investor's backing and contacts, the business continues to prosper, and sales soar to 2 million dollars in the third year. Once again, cash flow is tight. The inventor-entrepreneur requests an urgent meeting with the investor, confident that the additional funds will be supplied.

"Mr. Investor, we have been doing splendidly! Profits are far beyond our projections due to increased sales and the improved management and controls provided by your people. But we now need an additional $500,000."

After a meaningful pause the investor replies, "Let me refer you to our original deal. You were told, not once but several times, to ask us at that time for all the investment you would *ever* need. Otherwise, we would have to reconsider. Now, we cannot make a further investment unless we have a controlling interest."

The 'Run' is now in place.

At this point, the inventor-entrepreneur exclaims angrily, "I'd rather see the company fail than give up controlling interest. So, I'll just bankrupt it!"

The investor replies, "You do what you have to do. If

necessary we are prepared to lose the funds invested. But don't make a decision now. We are in no hurry. Let us know your plans as soon as you can."

The inventor pours his heart out to his wife that night as he paces the floor. He proclaims again and again how he will just let the business go under. She listens and assures him of her complete support, whatever he decides to do. Across town, the investor sleeps well, confident that the inventor's love for his creation will not permit him to file for bankruptcy protection.

A few days later a subdued entrepreneur meets with the investor. The value of the stock is updated to include earnings of the third year of operations. The $500,000 is paid in and the investor is issued additional shares of common voting stock equivalent to 60 percent of the company, leaving the inventor with 40 percent total interest. Additional key management and technical people are brought into the firm and the original owner is rarely consulted.

The business prospers and the following year again requires additional working capital. The investor notifies the inventor that an additional $500,000 is needed and that his pro-rata share is $200,000.

"But, I don't have that kind of money!"

"If you can't come up with your pro-rata share of the new funds, we will have to purchase additional shares and dilute your interest accordingly."

And so it goes. A year or so later, the original owner's interest is less than 10 percent, a small slice of the big pie. At some point the entrepreneur decides -- or is pressured -- to sell the remaining interest to the investor, often receiving enough to live comfortably the rest of his or her life. This settlement is not due to any generosity on the part of the investor, but comes from an awareness that a belligerent and persistent minority shareholder can be a significant detriment.

And so the inventor-entrepreneur, who would have endangered his very life to protect his 'baby', is finally divested of all he holds dear. In his bitterness he tells anyone who will listen how, "Those *!%?!!* investors stole my company!"

Fortunately, there are valid ways to protect against the Bump-and-Run strategy and make the Bad Guys -- in this case the investors -- finish last, or at least not ahead of the entrepreneur. These will be discussed in a subsequent chapter.

Not A Risk-Taker

Outsiders tend to view entrepreneurs as individuals who take risks, who plunge -- willy-nilly -- into new ventures. They are regarded as somewhat reckless, often flamboyant. The reality is that they are not risk-takers, but people who carefully assess the pros and cons of a project, measure and evaluate the possible downside, identify the market niche, then deliberately and judiciously become the authors of well-planned, purposeful innovations.

It is true that some so-called entrepreneurs do not know what they are doing and violate the most basic rules of business. They are not prepared. They do not do their due diligence. These relatively few may have fixed the image of entrepreneurs, in the public perception, as risk-takers.

Personal Evaluation Checklist

There are detailed personality profiles and evaluations compiled by leading authorities in psychology and human resources and relations. Their findings are supported by exhaustive studies that can be very meaningful and valuable. They use formulas and variables in varying degrees of difficulty which may be hard, if not almost impossible, for the layman to comprehend and implement. But, the reader might find some of them valuable.

There are also detailed lists of attributes, characteristics and habits of entrepreneurship which can be helpful in a self-evaluation.

For simplicity's sake, the author has created an overall *Personal Evaluation Checklist* for the reader's use.

A. Begins with questions regarding employment. This is mainly to define the career path now being followed, and the aptitude of the individual to enter the field of entrepreneurship. It is not per se subject to a rating scale.

B. The second section is a list of attributes designed to permit self-evaluation. It is not definitive, nor scientific, but is provided as a vehicle to assess one's entrepreneurial attributes as of the moment. A low 'score' on *My Average Attributes Rating* section may or may not be meaningful.

C. Complete the questionnaire again at 6 months after working on entrepreneurial attribute development.

Studies have shown conclusively that the majority of individuals can learn to be entrepreneurs. In addition to courses in many two and four year colleges, there are private Centers for Entrepreneurial Studies and Management, such as the one directed by Joseph R. Mancuso.

See "Additional References" at the end of this chapter.

PERSONAL EVALUATION CHECKLIST

A. **MY PERSONAL CAREER PATH OR BACKGROUND**
(Please check the boxes most applicable to you)
- ☐ Is mainly in privately held small or medium-sized companies.
- ☐ Is mainly in public corporations.
- ☐ Is in other large corporations or institutions.
- ☐ I am comfortable in the corporate environment.
- ☐ I do not like the corporate environment but 'play the corporate game' well.
- ☐ I am basically unhappy in the corporate structure.
- ☐ I work better with my superiors than with my peer group.
- ☐ I relate better to my peers and underlings than to my superiors.

B. **ENTREPRENEURIAL ATTRIBUTES - SELF EVALUATION**
(Circle the number which is most applicable in each line)

		(Ask an associate to complete)
Attributes	**How I View Myself**	**How Others View Me**
a. Self-Starter	1 2 3 4 5 6 7 8 9 10	1 2 3 4 5 6 7 8 9 10
b. Leadership	1 2 3 4 5 6 7 8 9 10	1 2 3 4 5 6 7 8 9 10
c. Organized	1 2 3 4 5 6 7 8 9 10	1 2 3 4 5 6 7 8 9 10
d. Management	1 2 3 4 5 6 7 8 9 10	1 2 3 4 5 6 7 8 9 10
e. Creativity	1 2 3 4 5 6 7 8 9 10	1 2 3 4 5 6 7 8 9 10
f. Ingenuity	1 2 3 4 5 6 7 8 9 10	1 2 3 4 5 6 7 8 9 10
g. Commitment	1 2 3 4 5 6 7 8 9 10	1 2 3 4 5 6 7 8 9 10
h. Perseverance	1 2 3 4 5 6 7 8 9 10	1 2 3 4 5 6 7 8 9 10
i. Will Sacrifice	1 2 3 4 5 6 7 8 9 10	1 2 3 4 5 6 7 8 9 10
j. Marketing	1 2 3 4 5 6 7 8 9 10	1 2 3 4 5 6 7 8 9 10
k. Sales Ability	1 2 3 4 5 6 7 8 9 10	1 2 3 4 5 6 7 8 9 10

Attribute Rating Totals (a-k)   **A** ☐   **B** ☐

Combine **A** and **B** totals and divide (A + B) by 2.

My Average Attributes Rating is: ☐

55-65 Fair.   65-75 Good.   75-85 Very Good.   85-100 Excellent.

(In-depth methods of Personality Evaluation - See References - end of Chapter One).

The "Creative Innovations" Attribute

Lifelong amassing of knowledge from experience, observation and a variety of seemingly unrelated sources can create an amazing storehouse from which technologies can be combined for creative enhancements to existing products or innovative new products or services. The mind of the venturer constantly probes for possible products and market niches in light of all the accumulated knowledge.

Illustration Capsule One

On a recent flight I observed flight attendants as they struggled with the heavy, unwieldy food and beverage cart. I knew that airlines have been sued for resultant back injuries. There is obviously a *need* for an improved cart. The thinking process began, outlined on the back of an envelope.

"Project: To replace heavy, unwieldy metal food and beverage carts with lighter ones of molded fire-resistant plastic, with indents to spare passenger elbows. Carts should be electric, with push-bar control of brakes, and controlled by a wire or tape concealed under the aisle carpet. The necessary technology already exists. Note: Whether such a new product and methodology is warranted will depend on requirements for sealed motors, as well as FAA and other necessary approvals. Also, power source location and weight will be a factor."

Illustration Capsule Two

I browsed through a magazine, found an article about housing difficulties for the elderly, and the economic and physical need for families to continue living in the same house. The creative process began anew.

"Project: Develop a free-standing, factory-built Mother-in-Law Apartment. Possibly of geodesic design. Name it 'Mother-in Law Pod'? Must have all amenities including kitchen, living-dining area, bedroom and bath. Special electric-powered wheel chair which, at the touch of a button (using warehouse forklift technology), will follow a magnetic tape under the carpet either to the kitchen, the bedroom or the bathroom. Use wheelchair unit -- already in production -- which allows a person to 'stand' upright, even though legs will not support the body. Then the mother-in-law can wheel her power chair into the kitchen, touch a button and be raised erect. This will provide a powerful psychological boost because, once vertical, she can prepare meals and feel almost normal."

The brainstorming continued. "Parents and in-laws inevitably become enfeebled, yet should be able to take a normal bath, luxuriating in a tub, and not a sitting bath. Design attachments for both wheelchair and tub which will position a person over the tub and gently lower him or her to a sitting, then a gradually reclining position and reverse at the touch of buttons." I scribbled some numbers. "A comfortable pod could be built and sold for $30,000 to $50,000. Long-term financing is needed. Once a door is cut into a wall of the children's home, and the pod fastened to the structure, it will qualify for FHA and other long-term financing. When the parents die, the pod can easily be removed."

The typical entrepreneur considers one or more possible applications almost daily. A few of these ideas stand immediate scrutiny and are researched. Most are discarded for reasons of marketing, timing or onerous and expensive government regulation requirements (as in the case of the contemplated new food and beverage airline cart).

There is no scientific theory of creative innovation, but we know that inquiring minds constantly seek innovative opportunities. It is an important skill to develop, and a rare gift to learn systematic innovation. The key is to recognize and identify an apparent need, verify what improvements might be introduced for a better product or service. The best new products or services may well emerge from the unexpected, even the apparently incongruous, to better meet a perceived product or service need.

ADDITIONAL REFERENCES

Clifford M. Baumbach and Joseph R. Mancuso: *Entrepreneurship and Venture Management;* Second Edition (Prentice-Hall, 1987). See *"Stage One-The Entrepreneur's Early Development"* (pp 1-3).

Robert Benfari, PhD: *Understanding Your Management Style:* (Lexington Books, 1991). A thorough analysis of personality measurement beyond MBTI. Valuable in-depth evaluation of personality and management styles.

Peter F. Drucker: *Innovation and Entrepreneurship -- Practice and Principles*; (Harper & Row, 1985). Deep Insight from the master. Emphasis on Internal Corporate Entrepreneurs.

Fred Klein: *Handbook on Building A Profitable Business*; (Entrepreneurial Workshop Publications, Seattle, 1990). A comprehensive self-test of 120 questions to help you determine your personality and management style.

Jeffry A. Timmons: *The Entrepreneurial Mind;* (Brick House Publishing Company, 1989). See Chapter 8 *"What Skills Are Needed"* for an extensive self-evaluation checklist.

Joseph Schumpeter: *The Theory of Economic Dynamics,* 1911. Reference to J. B. Say and early definitions of the *entrepreneur.*

Peter F. Drucker *Innovation and Entrepreneurship -- Practice and Principles;* (1985). Introduction: Declares that entrepreneurship truly emerged in the previous 10 to 15 years and produced 35 million jobs while large corporations created 5 million.

Notable Quotes from Peter F. Drucker

"The practice of Innovation: Innovation is the specific tool of entrepreneurs, the means by which they exploit change as an opportunity for a different business or a different service. It is capable of being presented as a discipline, capable of being learned, capable of being practiced. Entrepreneurs need to search purposefully for the sources of innovation, the changes and their symptoms that indicate opportunities for successful innovation. And they need to know and to apply the principles of successful innovation."

"Entrepreneurship is not a personality trait. In 30 years I have seen people of the most diverse personalities and temperaments perform well in entrepreneurial challenges. To be sure, people who need certainty are unlikely to make good entrepreneurs. Everyone who can face up to decision-making can learn to be an entrepreneur and to behave entrepreneurially.

Entrepreneurship then, is behavior other than personality trait. And its foundation lies in concept and theory rather than in intuition."

"They that will not be counselled cannot be helped. If you do not hear reason, she will rap you on the knuckles."
- *Benjamin Franklin*

CHAPTER TWO |

THE LAW OF THE HALF-BOOT - STARTING UP

It has been said that, *"An employee's value is the same to one company as it is to another."* In other words, ability, know-how, and experience qualify him or her for a lateral move to other firms at a similar level of responsibility, with the same or somewhat better compensation. The obvious reality is that, during periods when companies are not hiring, this maxim is of little comfort to those terminated because of mergers, downsizing, etc. Many become involuntary entrepreneurs. They are forced into starting their own ventures or to purchase struggling companies. Others take temporary refuge in unemployment compensation, and may ultimately become resigned to lower-paying jobs. A few with sufficient resources may 'purchase a position' as a condition for making a relatively modest investment (usually $20,000 to $30,000) in small closely-held companies in urgent need of capital and management. Still others become consultants to small and medium-sized companies.

The Law of the Half-Boot

We have seen that termination of employment in large private and public corporations creates many involuntary entrepreneurs. Employees are often fired for breaking what I call the *Law of the Half-Boot*, which is usually not a written 'law' but is nonetheless real and inexorably enforced. It takes many forms and is most prevalent in privately-held corporations. Violations of the sometimes eccentric, nearly phobic, and seemingly inconsequential policies of any given company sooner or later create *Involuntary External Entrepreneurs*. Dismissal will inevitably occur -- usually sooner than later.

The following Case Studies, each of which is as true as memory permits, will illustrate (better than a written explanation) how this *Law of the Half Boot* works:

Illustration Capsule One

Name: Company X • Los Angeles, California.
Description: Manufacturer • Public Corporation.
Control: Nominally controlled by the former sole owner, still the President.
Urgent Need: New Vice President for Manufacturing.
Policies: It is an unwritten law that every executive will dress in conservative dark suit, white shirt and tie, and polished black Oxfords.

Scenario: A top-notch executive was recruited as a vice president. He proved to be the right choice, but the President noticed that the VP insisted on wearing half-boots, saying that they supported his ankles. The truth was that he loved his half-boots, believing they brought him good luck. The president initially overlooked this lack of compliance, hoping that time would cause the new executive to see the light.

A year later the president interviewed the VP, asked him why he was not more of a 'team player', why he refused to set a good example to others in the company. That, though obedient to most of the rules and policies, he still insisted on wearing his zippered half-boots. The VP still refused to mend his ways and join the other employees in their standard shiny black Oxfords. His employment was abruptly terminated, although his contributions to the business were substantial.

"I guess I violated the *Law of the Half-Boot*," he was quoted as saying with a rueful smile.

Illustration Capsule Two

Name:	Steel Company • San Francisco.
Description:	Steel Fabricator • Private Corporation.
Control:	Sole Owner.
Urgent Need:	Recruit an Export Manager.
Policies:	Executives are not expected to drive a car newer than the owner's four year-old Ford. Profit-sharing and equity ownership are taboo.

Scenario: The company president decided to create a new Export Department to expand the company's market for a line of utility buildings and steel sash. I was hired to organize and manage the new Export Department. At the end of the first year, earnings were substantial. The "Old Man" surprised me with a generous bonus, which I used to purchase a new Buick convertible... the first violation of the Law of the Half-Boot.

It seemed a good time to ask for a substantial increase in salary, which was granted without comment. I became the second-highest paid executive in the company... second violation of the Law of the Half-Boot.

During the second year of employment it seemed only fair that I share in the net profits of the Export Department. Though the owner grumbled, he verbally agreed -- to my delight -- to pay me 7 percent of the annual net profits of the department. I was newly married and our dream home was being designed... the third and final violation of the Law of the Half-Boot.

November arrived. I was called to the old man's office and met the vice-president in the hall. "Your days are numbered," he said with evident relish. The president's lower lip was thrust out, his thumbs and forefingers twiddling with both ends of a yellow pencil and his head retracted turtle-like between his shoulders. As he studied the twirling pencil, only the top of his head was visible. With the inevitable awareness of detail that accompany such moments, I counted five carefully combed traversing wisps of hair that seemed glued to his otherwise bald pate. Danger signals flashed.

"How much will we owe you next month?"

I named the fairly substantial amount and added, "We had a very successful year in the Export Department, as you know."

"But," I hastily added, "I certainly do not feel strongly about it. Would you prefer to adjust the amount?"

Not so much as moving his head or looking up, he replied, "Nope! Not one red cent! For what I would have to pay you next month, I can get an Export Manager for two years!"

Stabbing the pencil in the air, he said, "Instead of climbing the ladder one rung at a time -- and if a rung breaks you keep climbing upward -- you shot up like a rocket!" The pencil emphasized the trajectory.

"You're fired!"

I walked slowly to the building a few blocks away where my new bride managed an IBM tabulating unit (precursor of the computer) for the U.S. Army Corps of Engineers.

"What are you doing here so early?" she asked.

"The Old Man just fired me."

I had violated the *Law of the Half-Boot* -- not once -- but three times, and the price was inevitably exacted.

Illustration Capsule Three

Name: Property Investment Group • San Francisco.
Description: Real Estate Investment and Management.
Control: Closely-Held Private Company.
Urgent Need: Recruit a Leasing Manager.
Policies: A rigid line of authority. Executives protected their turf. Middle level executive always felt threatened.

Scenario: The Company had recently acquired the Los Angeles World Trade Center. A dynamic young man with little formal business experience, but with a unique knack for quick learning, was hired as the Leasing Manager. Within a matter of months, he substantially increased leasing revenue in the Center and was asked to manage the corporate office building as well as two shopping centers.

Eager to advance in the company, he suggested ways to improve efficiency and profitability -- all of which were ignored by his supervisor, who, soon thereafter, became ill and was out of the office for several weeks. During his absence, the Leasing Manager acted on several of his previously ignored recommendations, which resulted in immediate and long-term benefits to the company. When his superior returned to the office and found what had been done without his approval, he informed top management that, "He is not a team player."

These have always been fashionable words to accelerate the departure of an employee. Several weeks later, the Executive checked his supervisor's daily calendar. He noted that a new man had been employed and placed in charge of all the projects of the former Leasing Manager.

After at least two violations of the *Law of the Half-Boot*, the price -- as always -- had to be paid. After further corporate immersion, he is now an accomplished entrepreneur, the sole owner of a multimillion dollar film conversion and packaging export business.

Before accepting employment in any corporation, be it large or small, private or public, it is always worthwhile to talk to former employees about its written and unwritten policies and idiosyncrasies. This knowledge can help avoid unintentional violations of the *Law of the Half-Boot* , and premature induction into the ranks of involuntary entrepreneurs.

Yes, the Law of the Half-Boot is alive and well.

How to Begin the New Venture

Characteristics of an entrepreneurial venture are: (1) a need is identified, (2) a product or service market niche is evaluated and validated, and (3) *added value* is created in a new or existing enterprise. Starting a business where new value is added is almost always entrepreneurial. Acquiring a retail business with an existing customer base where it is difficult to add value (travel agency, automotive repair shop, quick-copy store, flower shop, etc.) may or not meet the criteria for entrepreneurship. It is rarely possible to create new markets or devise new products or service applications in such entities. Little new value is created. Sales may increase due to new management style and personality or better use of resources and more creative advertising, but the basic business entity remains the same.

Basic Requirements

Those starting a new business need to know certain basic requirements including:

a. Location for the new business.

b. Applicable tax law and city, county, state, and other federal laws and regulations.

c. Business tools: profit-and-loss, cash flow projections and business plans.

d. Computer literacy as to word processing and spread-sheets.

e. Presentation and communication skills.

f. Ability to envision alternate products or services.

g. Ability to turn adverse situations to advantage.

h. Nearly every business is inadequately financed; the key is to maximize available resources.

i. A product or service must be timely and viable as determined by the available market.

Location for the New Business
A basic rule of real estate is that the three most important requirements for a project are: "Location. Location. Location." This is applicable to start-up enterprises as well. There are two common errors in business site selection. The first is the human tendency to select a location on a 'gut-feeling', on

the basis of impulse rather than due diligence.

There is something about the sight of a vacant storefront in an otherwise fully-leased shopping center that triggers feelings of optimism and need for ownership. But, it rarely pays to try to adopt a specific space to a business. The needs of the business should govern the selection of suitable space.

Example: During the past decade, three attempts have been made to open an ice cream store in a small strip shopping center near my home. Ignoring reality, the last owner, like the previous two, "just knew" it would be a prime location for an ice cream shop. Yet, even the most modest market survey would have indicated there is no real market niche. Within a year he joined the lament of his predecessors: *"To heck with the cheese. Let me out of the trap!"*

Within a radius of 5 miles, two similar businesses flourish. There is no apparent reason why consumers of frozen treats prefer to drive to these less attractive places of no better quality or price. They just do. A fourth candidate will probably come forward to reopen that ice cream shop. This is the *law of the next optimist* and the lifeblood of the business broker.

The second most common error is to select an overly expensive location and appoint it with costly furniture and fixtures to acquire a perceived status and dignity for the new enterprise, when it is not really indicated. There is no need, for example, to locate a drop-ship wholesale catalog sporting goods business (where the manufacturer ships direct to the customer) in an expensive office building. Because, by the very nature of catalog sales, buyers rarely visit the place of business. The owner goes to the customers. A small office and a post office box would be sufficient.

The true entrepreneur rarely feels the need for ostentation

or even creature comfort. Many owners of small manufacturing companies continue to work out of cramped, Spartan offices, in spite of the fact that their business is flourishing. Of course, if the start-up business depends on walk-in or drive-in trade, the space must be in a well-visited location and be attractive and inviting.

A Premise is to lease the lowest cost space suitable for first and perhaps second year operations. Storage mini-warehouses or business incubators (discussed in a later chapter), are often a good initial solution.

As the business grows, expandable flex-space, such as warehouse and/or manufacturing area with adjunct offices, may be warranted. As the venture expands, the decision whether to lease, build or buy property becomes important. If working capital is tied-up in the too-early acquisition of a building, it could be a fatal blow to the business.

It might, however, be advantageous to build or buy a building if a modest down payment can be made from discretionary funds, and monthly mortgage payments are the same or slightly more than equivalent rent or lease payments. Assuming the selection of owned space is in a good location, there is an opportunity for property to appreciate.

Applicable Tax Law and City, County, State and Other Federal Laws and Regulations

If a location looks too good to be true, it probably is. It is vital to ascertain in advance if proposed operations are possible at the proposed site. Zoning and deed restrictions may limit the use. And, there may be an insurmountable burden of regulatory caveats as federal, state, county and city agencies -- which habitually swell upon their granted authority --

become *Bad Guys*.

The Food and Drug Administration (FDA) can be a real bogeyman. Even if a new product has a verified market niche, if it is found to be subject to FDA approval, one might be advised to develop an alternate product to avoid the extreme costs and delays of obtaining said approvals. It is not uncommon for companies to spend tens of thousands of dollars and devote many months, often years to this process.

Also ready to be Bad Guys are: various Water Authorities ("Sorry, your property has just been reclassified to wetlands,") the U.S. Army Corps of Engineers ("The impact study will *only* take 6 months to a year,") and the Environmental Protection Agency ("There are buried tanks of solvents under your building lot. You can't build until it's cleaned up.") In addition, there are OSHA, city and county commissions, building and fire departments and others, all with veto power over the start-up. There are many horror stories of companies installed at considerable cost, which never begin operating because such agencies aggressively apply their interpretation of rules and regulations. It is interesting, but not surprising, that while these government agencies were originally created for the greater good of the community (and indeed have done much to promote clean water and healthy, uncontaminated earth and atmosphere), they have often pushed the outer limits of their original empowerment. It's when these agencies swell on their authority and stifle new businesses that they must be considered *Bad Guys*.

In our over-regulated communities, these *business contaminants* seem to be everywhere. Typically staffed with consummate bureaucrats who enjoy nearly unlimited power, they frequently exhibit a jaundiced attitude, tinged with jealousy, toward the world of business. An unknown author once described public employees' view of business as follows:

> *"(They are) like so many gray-green trolls under a gray-green bridge, fighting over the last moldy gray-green piece of cheese."*

Laws and regulations designed to protect endangered animals, birds, and plants tend to stifle creation of new businesses, if over-zealously applied. In central Florida, for instance, an endangered scrub jay subspecies, if observed flitting across your property, is enough to halt development. Thus, owners of vacant land tend to keep their land denuded to discourage the little bird from visiting. Well-meaning authorities have cleared land of stands of trees to provide scrub jay habitat, and are embarrassed that the jay does not move in. At the same time, they have removed picnic tables to discourage visitors in at least one local park, because scrub jays came to indulge their passion for peanuts.

Several years ago, another tiny bird, a species of flicker, caused millions of dollars of damage and delay by pecking over 100 holes in the insulation of the Space Shuttle as it stood ready for launch. NASA officials were paralyzed at first by a 'fear-to-offend' local environmentalists, but finally took steps to discourage the birds' enthusiastic drilling.

Evolution of Regulatory Pollution

It is my personal belief -- garnered from the study of history and decades of firsthand observation -- that our burgeoning regulatory *pollution* is not due so much to bad intent as to the inevitable result of elapsed time. For more than 200 years of our great nation's existence, our legislative, quasi-legislative and administrative bodies have striven to create new laws, rules and regulations to respond to changing conditions. Indeed, their creators' stature (at least in Congress) is measured in large part by the number of bills successfully sponsored and voted into law. Ever-increasing restrictive and regulatory impediments are a natural by-product of our country's aging process. This is not surprising, as it is a known fact that bureaucratic overburden pollutes all older societies.

Example: In one Latin American nation, after being notified that an unspecified gift awaited me at the *Aduana,* (Customs), I spent the day buying official stamps, walking a set of documents back and forth to be signed, initialled and stamped, completing *trámites (TRAW-me-tays)* -- a wonderful Spanish word with no one-word English equivalent that means bureaucratic 'make-work' requirements.

After completing 12 trámites in as many different offices, an exorbitant duty was assessed. I insisted on seeing my gift before paying the duty. It turned out to be a stale box of chocolates from a well-meaning friend in the United States. I bowed and handed the battered package to the stony-faced custom's officer, *"Que lo disfrute!"* ("Enjoy!")

It is rare for an older country to strip-off regulatory overburden accumulated over centuries, and to return to its entrepreneurial origins. New nations rarely invent regulatory burden, because of their need to create infrastructure and gross national product. The good news is that with all our regulatory woes, we have not (yet) reached the level of bureaucratic burden common to many other nations in Europe and Latin America.

Profit-and-Loss and Cash Flow Projections

One of the most important business tools for the new enterprise is the business plan, with accompanying profit-and-loss and cash flow projections. Many owners and managers of new businesses shy away from (or are too impatient with) the business plan concept. Ignorant of the elements and benefits of such a plan, and/or untrained in its use, they often do not know either their 'markups' or costs. One exception is illustrated in an anecdote:

"Billy-Bob, you have a profitable junk business. How do you do it, when you can neither read nor write?"

"Well, Ah buys for $1.00 and Ah sells for $4.00, and that *3 percent purely adds up.*"

With such a "3 percent" (actually 300 percent) markup this business needs no business plan. But most do. There are easily understood, straightforward books in nearly every library which detail how to create business plans, profit-and-loss statements and cash flow projections. For the computer-literate, inexpensive software programs are available which follow a step-by-step format, but they may suffer from an overkill of detail.

Projections for 1, 2, 3 and even 5 years can be laboriously prepared by hand with a calculator, as they nearly all were until a decade ago, prior to the widespread use of the personal computer. Large green-lined pads are still available providing for 15 or more columns (for months, subtotals and totals), and up to 100 rows (for sales, direct costs, indirect costs, fixed and variable sales, administrative expenses, etc.).

However, a model projection prepared by hand is cumbersome and cannot easily be used for 'what-if' scenarios. In contrast, a computer spreadsheet will, after all direct and indirect costs and fixed and variable expenses are entered -- using a recurring formula -- instantly display both the projected Net Profit Before Taxes (NPBT) and the cash flow needs monthly and annually. So, *what if* sales might be lower and costs higher? No problem. The new figures are keyed-in, columns and rows change instantly, and revised profits (or losses) along with cash requirements, are forecast almost immediately.

It is important in the start-up phase of a new enterprise that the entrepreneur learn -- if at all possible -- at least minimal keyboard (typing) skills and become computer-literate in spreadsheets and word-processing. Personal computers (IBM-compatible or Apple Macintosh) and printers are affordable for any business owner, and often come with word processing and spreadsheet programs already installed. Almost any generic spreadsheet software program will suffice for projection purposes. Most have evolved from the formulas of Visicalc. Software programs for word processing, invoice preparation, mailings, check writing, mail-merge, etc. are inexpensive, ubiquitous and mostly user-friendly.

Author's note: An early spreadsheet program for personal computers was *Visicalc*. Prior to the advent of the first IBM PC® in the early 1980's, this program was typically operated on a Model II, Tandy (Radio Shack)® personal computer at a hardware/software cost of from $7,500 to $8,500. Although ingenious, Visicalc had an unfriendly user's guide. To learn *replicate* and *ranges* concepts (i.e., to cause subsequent columns and rows on the spreadsheet to automatically compute from a formula applied to the first column and row) required a true gift of discernment. One could have wished for a Biblical *Urim and Thummin* in order to translate it.

Should the entrepreneur not feel comfortable with business plan preparation and the supporting profit-and-loss and cash flow projections, there are financial and business consultants who will, for a fee, provide these basic business tools and update them as needed. Accountants or CPAs are reluctant to generate such reports because it is not cost-effective for them, and is alien to their main professional activity, which is reporting the past, not forecasting the future.

The entrepreneur should not only become familiar with computers but, where possible, learn to perform *all* the operations of the budding enterprise. Today there are many viable, easy-to-use spreadsheet programs.

Ability to perform financial, administrative, marketing, sales, production and clerical tasks, will help make the entrepreneur self-reliant. Then, as the business grows, the owner is never completely dependent on any employee. It is beneficial for each employee to be aware that the owner-manager can do his or her job in an emergency.

Example: For many years, one of my tests of a new secretary or administrative assistant, as they are now usually designated, was to dictate a letter. If the letter came back to me for signature with errors and/or carelessly corrected 'strikeovers', I turned to my typewriter or computer, produced the letter error-free, signed and placed it in the out-basket. A few minutes later the employee was back in my office.

"This is not the letter I typed."

"That's right," I would respond quietly with a disarming smile. From that moment, every letter placed on my desk for signature was error-free, or carefully corrected.

Presentation and Communications Skills
Of the hundreds of entrepreneurs I have known, most were

able -- in one way or another -- to communicate the basic concepts required to market their new or improved product or services and to obtain needed resources. For instance, it is relatively easy to obtain credit from vendors. They are basically optimistic and usually only seek modest assurance of payment for materials or services. And, if the product or service fills a specific need, customers do not require a great communicator. Likewise, bankers are less interested in the communication skills of the owner of a venture than they are in assets and ability to repay the loan. Thus, it's not surprising to find that -- except for the most eccentric, introverted and withdrawn individuals -- an entrepreneur's dedication, willingness to learn, enthusiasm and belief in a niche-filling product or service will usually suffice to obtain needed resources and customers.

Being able to communicate ideas and make good presentations, however, is of great importance to the ultimate success of an enterprise. To achieve or refine this attribute, the entrepreneur will need to practice. Like Demosthenes, one of history's great orators, who overcame a speech impediment by speaking for countless hours to an imaginary audience with his mouth full of pebbles, the entrepreneur can learn more effective communication by trial, error and practice.

Ability to Envision Alternate Products or Services

Entrepreneurs must have the creative ability to develop alternate products or services and additional markets in the event the initial venture's niche does not materialize as planned.

Illustration Capsule One

A number of years ago, three investors organized a company to manufacture acrylic (plexiglass) gift items such as breakfast trays, gift boxes, novelties, etc. One shareholder supplied raw materials from his plastics scrap company, mainly low-cost acrylic offcuts. My small investment company provided financing and general management. The third shareholder was a skilled plastics technician/plant manager.

Production began, but the market failed to develop. It was necessary to either close the business or develop new markets. As an emergency measure to provide positive cash flow, we purchased two sets of wood molds at a bargain price for three-dimensional 12- and 24-inch vacuum-formed plastic letters, and began an intensive local marketing effort. Soon, nearly every company in the area displayed their names on the front wall of their buildings, in three-dimensional acrylic vacuum-molded letters in bright colors.

With the resultant cash infusion, we created a new product; discontinued the manufacture of discretionary consumer products. We designed patterns and manufactured molds for products needed in the housing industry; clear acrylic sky domes, vacuum-formed plastic bi-fold closet doors, vanities, and a series of indoor and outdoor lights. The business became successful and the shareholders benefited from the income tax-exempt sale of the firm, 5 years later, to a public company.

Ability to Turn an Adverse Situation to Advantage

The entrepreneur, though not a taker of risks per se, is generally optimistic and self-confident by nature.

Illustration Capsule Two:

Years ago, I provided management consulting services to a group of real estate investors. One of their projects was a motel at an intersection with I-95 in Central Florida. The other three corners of the intersection were vacant land. The motel project had been authenticated by a feasibility study prepared by a leading motel consulting firm. We were surprised to note, a month or so later, that land was being cleared to build another motel in the northeast quadrant. Within the year a third motel was constructed on the southwest corner. The market was over built.

How did this happen? Three motel consulting firms independently developed favorable feasibility studies for one motel each at the intersection. All three consultants later claimed that they had no knowledge of the other studies. The result? The tourist market was woefully inadequate to support the hundreds of rooms built. The owners of one motel sought protection under federal bankruptcy laws. Another was subsidized in various changes of ownership, until natural market growth and tourism increased occupancy rates to profitability.

There were few alternate uses for a low-occupancy motel. My clients, owners of the initial motel, enhanced their cash flow by converting units to cottage industries and offices until, finally, the growing tourist market brought profitability to all three motels. This was the best solution available at the time. Today, there are companies which specialize in converting such properties to attractive mini-storage warehouse spaces financed by pension funds. A prime example is the *Fontainbleu* motel in New Orleans. Processed through the RTC, it has been converted to an upscale mini-warehouse complex.

Many enterprises may, at any given time, defy the creation

of alternate products and/or services to supplant the originally-designated market when it caps out or fails to materialize. But the innovative entrepreneur will find ways to increase cash flow, if there is any alternate market niche at all, and be poised for future market innovations.

The Key is to Maximize Resources

It is true that there are successful entrepreneurs who have started their enterprises with "$50 or $100." But, most ventures require substantial amounts of start-up and ongoing working capital or credit. If the entrepreneur has savings, but little or no other income, it is impressive how fast the nest egg disappears in daily living expenses. And, should two entrepreneurs join in an enterprise and both require living wages, their combined savings vanish exponentially. Outside investors or lenders are understandably reluctant to provide capital to subsidize the entrepreneur's living costs. And there is always inertia in obtaining third party start-up funding for the enterprise, due to the high mortality rate of new businesses.

One solution for the owner is to keep his or her 'day-job' and not look to Newco for expenses or salary, while providing the effort necessary to make it a success. There are advantages to this approach. By providing 'sweat equity', initial sales translate to higher profits, which, if scrupulously reinvested in inventory, tooling, machinery and equipment, will result in lower production costs and increased profits, maximizing financial resources.

Illustration Capsule Three

Our filter manufacturing company had survived the 5-year business 'half-life' challenge and continued its profitable path. We adhered to the rule: *Maximize all resources,* but did not scrimp on tooling or profit-enhancing improvements in machinery and equipment. We were not tempted to spend for *wants* instead of *needs.* As investors, we knew that every dollar saved would be returned to us several times over in a 'times-earnings' formula when the time came to sell the company or its' assets.

I had begun to draw down my *sweat equity bank account,* accrued in previous years as off-the-books deferred compensation. Further, the company began paying monthly consulting fees to me and the majority shareholder.

The Company hired a full-time, *carrot-oriented* (a buzz-word from a fable about a burro spurred to action by a carrot dangled in front of its eyes) General Manager on the basis of estimated living expenses plus an incentive equity-sweetener (also called 'equity-kicker') of 20 percent of the common voting stock of the company, to be paid from his pro-rata share of annual profits.*

He became the major contributor to the ultimate success and sale of the business and capitalized his sweat equity handsomely when the business was sold.

As the business prospered, the level of accumulated retained earnings reached the danger zone. The 'magic figure' was approximately $250,000 in retained earnings. There were and still are strict limitations in the amount of permissible retained earnings. Substantial accumulated earnings make the IRS salivate, since it delays collection of the *double tax* on corporate earnings and dividends to shareholders.

The Bad Guys of IRS like to assess fines and penalties on such accumulations of capital, unless the funds are specifically designated to capital needs, etc. of the business. To forestall possible action by the IRS, the shareholders voted to recapture deferred compensation, and pay monthly consulting fees. The Exit Plan of the company did not mature at 5 years as planned, but assets of the company were finally sold after 8 years of operation, based upon six times the average annual earnings of the previous 3 years. The Return on Investment (ROI) was a very satisfactory 1670 percent (an annualized rate of 209 percent), an example of almost total maximization of modest resources and high NEBT (net earnings before taxes).

At the other end of the spectrum -- with strong financing an absolute necessity at the outset -- are entrepreneurial ventures with heavy capital requirements. From prototype to production model and market verification, often requires tens of thousands of dollars. In addition, the full time efforts of the entrepreneurs are not only necessary but critical, so that their living expenses must be covered until the new company becomes profitable. And, if marketing success propels it to a *fast-growth* mode, sophisticated second and third level private and/or public funding are a must.

These fast growing companies are the *entrepreneurial elite*. They are not within the expectations or even the purview of the average entrepreneur, but realized by only a select few. These fast-growth wonders are described in a quote from the fascinating book, *For Entrepreneurs Only*, by Wilson Harrell: *"...The entrepreneurs who run fast-growing companies (are) totally different in mind set..."* He continues with the theme that these are the self-styled buccaneers of entrepreneurship, who belong to what the author calls *The Club of Terror.* I never became a member of that club, and neither will the average entrepreneur. However, at one time or other, all entrepreneurs will become members of the *Anxiety Club.*

Between these two extremes -- ventures requiring only minimal capital resources, growing primarily from profits -- and those demanding substantial initial and ongoing resources -- there are, perhaps, nearly as many different types of entrepreneurial ventures as there are creative means of start-up and ongoing financing.

A New Product or Service Must be Timely

The fact that a product or service must be relevant and fill a specific market need is an obvious basic requirement that, amazingly, is often overlooked or ignored. Today, nearly anything that *can be sold* can be manufactured. Forty to fifty years ago, any new product created its own market. I smile at the recollection of a "guaranteed" flea exterminator which my grandfather ordered for the then substantial sum of $1. A small anvil arrived with a tiny hammer. The instructions read: "Place flea on anvil and strike smartly with hammer. Results guaranteed!"

Some inventors tend to fall in love with their creations which often have little marketable value. They blindly devote resources and energies to an unproven product, or one with doubtful market. I recall two would-be entrepreneur clients who developed a scissor-lift and received a design patent. No matter that similar scissor-lifts were already in use at airports for food services to airplanes, etc. They spent nearly $50,000 trying to market their 'invention'.

Sometimes the market is just not ready for the new product. When Philo T. Farnsworth, married to my mother's niece, first invented television, he was forced -- because of apathy in the U.S. -- to take the technology to Great Britain. Had he persisted in our national market, his limited resources would have probably doomed him to failure, and others would have overtaken him in television technology. As a later entrepreneur in the Capehart-Farnsworth television venture, he did well, but failed to truly reap the potential rewards of his invention.

I referred earlier to a business fabricating filter-strainers for wells with dirty water (sand, silt, shell, grit, etc.). Although there was a limited filter market in several states, the potential for sustained growth was there. Then, as drip irrigation came of age, this filter-strainer proved to be ideal for that market. The product was, unexpectedly, both timely and viable, as it kept the tiny emitters from clogging. It met the needs of this rapidly growing market.

*The author's son, who has reached significant heights of entrepreneurship.

"If we only begin, the mind becomes heated.
Only begin and the job is completed."
- *Anonymous*

CHAPTER THREE [

THE FLEDGLING BUSINESS

As previously noted, for more than 20 decades in the halls of our city, county, state and federal government agencies, diligent legislators and functionaries have layered thousands of rules, regulations and legislation relating to new businesses. In order to monitor compliance, a plethora of regulatory agencies has arisen. Our society has matured... aged in the wood of entrenched bureaucracy.

Given the limited resources of most new businesses -- often in the low-to-middle five figure range -- if they attempt from the outset to fully comply with all applicable Federal, state, county and municipal laws and regulations, resources can be used up even before the first product or service is sold.

In general, regulatory agencies are less than sympathetic. Their employees are 'just doing their job' to make certain the enterprise is organized *according to Hoyle.* *

The Early Entrepreneur May Get the Bird

Should full compliance be attempted in the early stages of the venture, thereby exhausting financial resources, it is the

---

Edmond Hoyle (1671-1769) English writer. His writings on the laws of the card game whist gave rise to the common phrase "according to Hoyle," signifying full compliance with universally accepted rules and customs.

entrepreneur who gets *the 'bird'*. Sometimes *deferred compliance* is necessary, and Hoyle must take a vacation.

There are a few enlightened exceptions to the above. A trend may be developing in a few community governments which, recognizing the need to create new jobs, address the obvious need to nurture start-ups and to provide assistance to the fledgling business with financial incentives, *deferred compliance* on costly regulations, and a tacit temporary moratorium on social levies. This allows the enterprise to bud and grow green shoots of modest profit. Once the roots of the business are established, the company is then strong enough for full compliance.

Illustration Capsule One

Joan Dinkins (not her real name) loved to look at a plaque inherited from her entrepreneur father inscribed, *"Build a better mousetrap, and the world will beat a path to your door."* Her father lived by that motto, and it worked for him in a time when nearly every new product was eagerly received.

Yet history has shown that there are better mousetraps gathering dust, while the homely, unchanging *el cheapo* is still produced in countries with the lowest labor rate.

Entrepreneurial like her father, Joan became increasingly aware of the limitations of her lipstick. Each morning, and several times during the day, she followed a ritual. First, she compressed her lips and applied lip rouge. Then she pressed upper and lower lip surfaces together in a sort of rolling motion, and branded a kiss-print on a sheet of facial tissue to remove the excess. Alas, a final check in the mirror often showed front teeth smeared with lipstick.

Joan was an insatiable reader. From accumulated knowledge, she combined known technology with a modicum of innovation, to create an ingenious applicator and lip rouge. The lip rouge was both heat-actuated and heat-sensitive. A prototype was made. It showed promise. As the applicator was drawn along the lip line, body heat caused the release of the proper thickness of applied rouge film. Where there was already a coating, it acted as a heat insulator, causing the applicator to stop dispensing. Then, where no lip gloss existed, normal body heat again triggered the even application of the proper amount of rouge. No smeared teeth.

Joan assembled her friends to demonstrate the production prototype. They were delighted with its performance, as well as the texture, color and taste of the new lip rouge. She began manufacturing the first 100 units in her garage, hand-built from shelf parts. A well-meaning friend at the local newspaper wrote a favorable article, complete with photographs. It was an exciting, fulfilling and rewarding moment -- until her doorbell rang.

"Ms. Dinkins? City Code Enforcement. We are informed that you are manufacturing in your garage in violation of city ordinances. We also received a complaint that there are several cars parked in front of your house during the day, which constitutes an unauthorized increase in vehicular traffic due to your business. You will have to desist." She was handed a Notice of Violation.

A few minutes later the doorbell rang again. An officious woman stood there. "I'm with the Office of Safety and Health Administration (OSHA). A complaint has been filed at our office about odors emanating from your garage. Are you manufacturing on the premises?"

The ensuing inspection resulted in Joan being cited for numerous additional violations.

The phone rang later that same day and she was informed that she must obtain valid city and county business licenses, and that, in any event, no licenses would be issued for manufacturing in her garage.

Then, in another phone call, came the crowning blow. "Ms. Dinkins? Jack Dredgewater of the Food and Drug Administration (FDA). You are making lip rouge without appropriate agency approvals. We are putting you on notice."

With dreams still alive, Joan set about to cure the violations. She was shocked to discover that tens of thousands of dollars and six months to a year would be required just to process the application and obtain necessary FDA approvals. The better applicator joined the better mousetrap on the shelf -- banished because the would-be entrepreneur was too optimistic, unprepared and unwary. Unfortunately, she was not aware of the respite offered by *deferred compliance*.

Illustration Capsule Two

An engineer with a Fortune 500 company in Florida, also owned a small landscaping business, which his wife managed, in order to augment their income. He noted that the shallow wells used for watering lawns brought up quantities of pump-damaging silt, sand, shell and grit. Filters available in the market were inadequate and difficult to clean. He invented and hand-built a few filter-strainers using off-the-shelf PVC fittings covered with clear polycarbonate covers. I contracted to manage the filter company as a consultant, and we elected a 'C-Corporation' to manufacture an improved product. Since my associate had no discretionary income, we opted to employ *deferred compliance* and *true sweat equity.* A new company was born -- not in a garage -- but in one small 10-feet by 10-feet storage bay at *Acorn Warehouses.*

The inventor/co-owner contributed assets to the company consisting of several small woodworking machines and a shelf inventory of PVC. I invested a minimal amount of cash and worked on a deferred fee-for-service basis. Our first action was to define the purpose and mission of the new venture, which was to build earnings as rapidly as possible, in order to capitalize by selling assets or corporate stock within 5 years.

During the first 2 years of operation, two-thirds of the filter-strainer market was in Florida. Our retail pricing for a standard 1-1/2 inch filter, with 60-mesh screened insert, was based upon a minimum gross profit of 40 percent of sales.

As a Premise for short and medium-run production, 40 percent is a favorable gross profit margin. For customized products, the minimum is 50 percent. And for custom (one-of-a-kind) products, the figure is from 60 to 100 percent (the latter in the jewelry trade is known as *one keystone).*

We selected a manufacturer's rep -- a commission sales agent. Small trial orders were booked for field testing, followed immediately by more substantial business.

In the second year we asked our manufacturer's rep to become a warehousing distributor. He was not interested. We arranged a one-year percentage override on area sales for his efforts in introducing the filter and the parting was amicable. Another manufacturing representaive firm agreed to be our warehousing distributor in the immediate market area, selling directly to wholesalers.

To achieve our share of the nationwide market, it was vital

to contract with leading warehousing (stocking) distributors. I soon discovered two basic criteria. First, our filters would be needed primarily where wells and surface water sources pumped so-called *dirty water*, contaminated with particulates of sand, grit, shell, silt, etc. Secondly, a growing drip irrigation market called for low-micron filtration to keep the tiny emitters from clogging.

The U.S. Department of Agriculture proved helpful, providing us with a detailed map of the United States. The map identified localities of dirty water, and listed areas where drip irrigation was taking hold. We talked with trade organizations, manufacturing reps and others, and soon identified the leading stocking distributors in applicable markets.

I personally prepared an exclusive warehousing distributor contract and used *mail-merge* in my computer to insert the name of each leading stocking distributor throughout the body of the agreement and on the signature page. A carefully worded cover letter was prepared, addressed by name to each owner or CEO, indicating that 'their company' had been selected as our exclusive warehousing distributor for their market area, and that signing, dating and returning one copy of the contract would constitute acceptance of the agreement. I signed each letter and mailed it with two copies of the proposed agreement, together with pricing sheets and technical data. Where there was one warehousing distributor servicing a given area, we sent one package. If there were two or more distributors in a major city, each received a package. The first distributor in each area, all things being equal, to return a signed copy of the agreement with an initial order for 500 filters, was granted the exclusive representation in its market area. Orders from that initial mailing totalled 2,500 filters.

The new warehousing distributor in northern California called to tell me, in no uncertain terms, of his displeasure. He had found out that our company had sent a signed contract to another distributor in his market area. My reply was succinct.

"Don, you have the exclusive representation, not your competitor. Okay?"

I was certainly glad he did not discover that we had sent not two, but a total of three identical pre-signed contracts to his area!

The original distributors established through that *single mailing* still account for 80 percent of the filter company's business. *Total initial marketing cost was less than $5,000.* Using traditional, non-creative marketing methods, the outlay would have been at least ten times that figure. *Marketing creativity often equates to conserving financial resources.*

Earnings from the first year of operations (with a small short-term loan assist from a local bank -- which was repaid in 6 months) paid for injection molds for the PVC filter bodies and polycarbonate covers. The resulting reduction in product cost was nearly threefold. Selling prices remained the same. The injection molds were amortized in less than 2 years. Substantial net profits before taxes (NPBT) up to 19 percent of sales were achieved regularly as sales increased, and we met and exceeded original goals. Assets of the company were ultimately sold for a total dollar amount in the high six figures.

Studies have indicated that there are an average of five new start-ups in the business life of an entrepreneur. In each of my five entrepreneurial ventures to date, I limited my total investment to discretionary funds to low-to-middle five figures. It was never in my nature -- and it never became necessary -- to mortgage the homestead.

Manufacturing Startup -- Initial Deferred Compliance

One solution to the hostile and costly regulatory environment is *initial deferred compliance* through various creative means, plus what might be called a *true sweat equity formula,* until the business achieves a solid financial base. A deferred compliance model is outlined below. Primarily applicable to manufacturing, it may be modified for other startups. *First, obtain all applicable city, county, and state business licenses.*

1. Keep the day-job to cover living expenses.
2. Employ no W-2 employees for the first year (or two), so there are *no* required filings or registration, and no direct outlays for levies such as Social Security, Workman's Compensation insurance, Unemployment taxes, etc. Use established Independent Contractors who are assessed lower social levy rates than your business.
3. Obtain basic fire and theft insurance. If possible, include business interruption insurance.
4. Keep the start-up tab of the new venture low.
5. Carefully monitor operating costs.
6. Take no salary, reimbursement of expenses, or other wages from the Company until the financial condition of the business permits.
7. Locate the new enterprise in a low-cost, low-profile production space, such as a mini-storage facility or Incubator space.
8. Energetically collect accounts receivable.
9. Bolster cash flow by negotiating extended credit from vendors.
10. Keep inventories to a minimum.

11. During first-level operations, don't identify the pro-
     duction location if it's in a mini-storage facility -- no
     sign on the door. Those who need to find the company,
     will. Those who don't, probably won't.
12. Avoid premature 'success story' articles in the media.
13. Limit advertising to the specific market.

This initial deferred compliance and cash flow-emphasis
formula builds net profits rapidly with the result that *ongoing
financial needs of the business are largely met from profits,
after provision for income taxes.*

The True Sweat Equity Formula

Throughout all my manufacturing enterprises, the *sweat
equity* business plan has worked well. A *true sweat equity*
formula might include the following:

(a) Invest minimal discretionary funds in start-up equity
     and/or loans.
(b) Defer payment for time and work contributions, in
     order to enjoy better exit equity appreciation.
(c) Defer reimbursement of out-of-pocket expenses.
(d) Take aggressive steps to minimize start-up expenses.
     Employ deferred compliance techniques.
(e) Severely limit administrative and marketing costs
     during the first level of operations.
(f) Contract with ICs (Independent Contractors) and Sub-
     contractors for production and other services.
(g) Through creative management, use every means pos-
     sible to maximize the available resources.
(h) As a policy, generate the best possible cash flow
     through high earnings.

(i) Apply net profits after income taxes *in toto* to capital improvements, servicing of accounts receivable, inventory, etc.

(j) Once a solid financial base is in place, begin full compliance with regulatory agencies.

(k) With increased profitability, begin to recoup deferred compensation.

(l) Implement the Exit Plan.

Suggested Initial Steps

1. <u>The Business Objective</u>

Decide the ultimate objective of the business, which could be one of the following:

(a) Build the Company to its first stage entrepreneurial limits. Capitalize by selling assets or equity, and set aside the resulting 'gelt' to start a second venture.

(b) Ramp the business up to the second stage by acquiring investors, and capitalize at a future date on the sale of the remaining retained equity.

(c) Move the business to a fast-growth mode via institutional debt and/or private or IPO (public stock offering).

(d) Take the company to the final stage -- the trustee and management level. Continue to build the business.

2. <u>The Product</u>

If the company is a manufacturing enterprise, consider the possibility of developing products attractive to warehousing (stocking) distributors -- either for the consumer or smokestack (industry) markets. Build a prototype, then a production model. Make a few handmade units and debug the product by field-testing it for 6 months or a year prior to start-up.

Achieve manufacturing cost reductions wherever possible, through design changes in the final product to enable the use of injection-molding, vacuum-forming, extruding, blow-molding, casting, machining on automatic or semiautomatic equipment, or other automated or semi-automated techniques.

Premise: These processes substantially lower production costs, which will, with no corresponding reduction in the selling price, dramatically increase net profits to service the ongoing financial needs of the business.

3. <u>Sales and Marketing</u>

Personally, or using a marketing consultant, make a low-cost preliminary market survey to identify the need and verify a market niche and potential for the product. Develop and validate the pricing structure to provide attractive margins at the stocking distributor and wholesale levels.

Premise: Selling to warehousing distributors might (or might not) reduce initial profit-taking, but certainly avoids costly initial and ongoing sales and marketing expenses.

4. <u>Selecting the Company Name</u>

After careful research, select a name for the new venture. When the entrepreneur selects -- for the first time -- a legal name for a new venture, a sense of happening, even excitement, pervades. It officially marks the end of one era and a new beginning. Name selection should, in most cases, be a process rather than a momentary, seat-of-the-pants decision. Several questions need to be asked. First, what should the name convey? Second, what acronym -- for name recognition -- is easily derived from the name? Third, what logo might be advantageously designed? It's not always necessary that the first letters of each word in a company name generate a meaningful acronym, but they often do. Combining the first two letters of the names of two or more owners might be just right -- or might not. Try it.

If the business is likely to have more than one type of customers, there may a need for two letterheads. A friend owns *The C. D. Group,* which stands for his two major business activities: *Church Development Group* or *Creative Design Group.*

Care should be taken to avoid names similar to easily recognized trade names, or names subject to misinterpretation, or any name that might be difficult to pronounce. I once recommended to my associates that, since our manufacturing venture in Puerto Rico was a *core industry* with several affiliates, we name it *Intercore Industries, Inc.* My joy in that name ended with the first few telephone calls. "Is this *Intercourse Industries?*" (followed by laughter). There was an emergency Board of Directors meeting. The new name became *Antilles Wood Industries, Inc.* with *AWICO* as its acronym.

I ultimately capitalized and fully-funded my 'gelt', i.e., capital that I would not touch, by selling my shares of common voting shares in *AWICO* to my associates -- Federal income *tax-free* -- at the second stage. The four of us had built and owned, in addition to the manufacturing company, two high-rise apartment buildings, a shopping center, and a housing project of 1,000 homes.

In passing, it is interesting to note that business names for consultants, such as *George Hill & Associates* or *The George*

Hill Group, usually means George is a sole practitioner, though he may use other specialists for specific tasks.

5. Main Office

Using initial deferred compliance as outlined above, I suggest that business letterhead and envelopes of the new manufacturing venture bear the home address of the entrepreneur as the *main office* of the enterprise. For the initial period, do all of the administrative office work at home. If there is insufficient room in the home, share an inexpensive office somewhere, but not at the manufacturing site. There should be no available space there anyhow.

Premise: Be reluctant to take deductions for business activity in your home. It's just not worth it. Such deductions often trigger unwelcome inquiries from the IRS.

6. Licenses

Obtain all necessary local and state licenses for business activity at the *home,* not the manufacturing location. In answer to the question as to what type of business will be conducted, I suggest selecting a non-threatening business category such as *business consultant* (you *are* a consultant to your own business), which usually gains ready approval. Zoning agencies usually seek assurance that traffic will not increase at the office location. If the community prohibits any type of home business at your residence, share the rent of a small office.

7. Legal Counsel

Select a reputable attorney to organize the legal structure of the company. Choose one who is actively working in business law and, preferably, affiliated with a law firm that has expertise in labor relations, tax law, and estate planning.

8. Legal Structure

With your attorney, decide which type of company might be the most advantageous legal form for your business. Whether it's a *Sole Proprietorship*, a *Subchapter S Corporation with a 1422 election (S-Corp)*, a *C-Corporation* (C-Corp), a *Limited Liability Company* (LLC), or a *Limited Partnership*, do not attempt to organize the legal business entity yourself. More about this in Chapter Four.

9. Accountant

Select a sole proprietor accountant for monthly operating and financial statements, and for the annual audited statements. *Once the business is on a solid path of growth, contract the annual audit to one of the major accounting firms.* The cost may be -- but often is not -- substantially higher. Bankers, investment bankers, private investors and potential buyers will have greater confidence and reliance in their reports.

10. Manufacturing Location

The mini-storage warehouse or industrial park.

Look for a mini-storage warehouse which, to improve occupancy and rate-of-return, also rents to small business owners. After checking with several of the current business tenants to verify that they have not been harassed by regulatory authorities, rent (on a one-year basis) one or more bays and install a telephone. Budding businesses in mini-storage warehouse spaces are usually ignored by regulators. This may be because they are difficult to regulate, usually nonproductive in terms of taxes and levies, and are often viewed as ephemeral and temporary. There's a sort of unwritten 'incubator' atmosphere that often -- but not always -- protects an entrepreneur at such locations from the local scions of social levies -- at least during the first level of operations.

(a) The Incubator

Another low-cost alternative might be to lease space in an *Incubator* facility. Incubators are either for-profit or not-for-profit entities, sometimes located in converted office buildings, but more often in flex-space clusters (one-story or low-rise buildings with offices in the front and warehouse/manufacturing space in the rear). Incubators typically offer favorable leases, the services of a secretary-receptionist, copier, fax machine and other services at a reduced rate, because they are pooled for a number of business entities. One disadvantage is that occupants of Incubator space present a higher profile -- making them more easily identified by curious regulators.

(b) The Garage

Many writers have chronicled the saga of the successful entrepreneur who "started making widgets in a one-car garage with only $100 (or was it only $10, or $1?) in his or her pocket," and then went on to become a multimillionaire manufacturer. There are, undoubtedly, still entrepreneurs who start out in a garage, but most do not. Except for rural areas, neighbors today are more prone to complain to city and local zoning officials about such things as an increase in traffic, increased noise and noxious odors. This triggers the attention of the regulatory Bad Guys. Against today's reality, the inventor-entrepreneur might hesitate to begin prototype production or first field-test manufacturing behind a garage door.

11. Signs

It is not necessary (unless marketing needs absolutely require it) to post a sign with the name of the company on the premises -- or even on the mailbox -- at the plant location during the start-up stage. The mailman, shipping and delivery people will find both addresses. There is no advantage to anyone else knowing the Company location. Note: In this manufacturing or resale of products scenario, 90 percent of sales will be to warehousing distributors -- people who may never visit the factory premises. This is the low-profile stage of the new business, where every penny saved goes to capital, and no *Bad Guy* alphabet-soup-agency distractions are needed.

12. IC Agreement: *1099s Forever... W-2s Almost Never*

If the new company has no employees for whom W-2 Forms must be filed, contributions for FICA (Social Security taxes), FUTA or SUTA (Federal and State Unemployment taxes), Workman's Compensation Insurance, etc. are not required. Make certain that all work performed meets the requirements for 1099 form filing. With no employees, the business is not legally required to register for any of the above social levies at this stage.

(a) Independent Contractors.

The entrepreneur should negotiate a contract with an *Independent Contractor* (IC) to produce, pack and ship the finished products, receive raw material, purchase parts and subassemblies, etc. During the first year of operations, the IC might even prepare invoices and sales orders as part of a fixed-price contract. Or, the entrepreneur can, in the start-up phase and with the help of a computer, personally handle purchases, vendor payments, etc. In an emergency, part-time help from personnel agencies can be employed. At the end of the taxable year, IRS Form 1099 is filed for payments to the Independent Contractors.

The IRS does *not* like the use of ICs. If IRS requirements are not met, the independent contractor relationship will be disallowed, with back taxes, penalties, fines, interest, and hassles to the entrepreneur as well as to the IC. In all probability, the IC will not meet *all* the criteria if audited by either Federal or state, so this is, at best, a temporary solution. (California's Employment Development Department, for example, is even more strict than the IRS). If requirements are not met, it can be difficult for the owner to prove that the IC is not an employee of the Company.

Create a thorough and detailed Independent Contractor Agreement. Research the requirements for yourself and pay careful attention to detailed and specific restrictions placed on such agreements by the IRS. The IC is usually a sole proprietor and is responsible for applicable employee payroll additions, and for reporting and filing and FICA, FUTA, SUTA contributions, etc. The entrepreneur is advised to monitor the IC to make certain it is current in such payments.

(b) Subcontractors

The manufacturing entrepreneur should use subcontractors wherever possible for subassemblies and process parts. The subcontractor assumes responsibilities for filing W-2s, Workmen's Compensation Insurance, Income Tax withholding, etc. for its employees, and is paid against presentation of invoices. Again, proper wording of the subcontract is absolutely essential. The IRS will try to assert that the 'sub' really acts as an agent of the owner, thereby causing the owner to be liable for a subcontractor's failure to comply with regulations.

13. Vendor "Cash Contributions"

Contact the comptroller or CFOs of several prime vendors to negotiate extended terms of credit for purchase parts and raw materials. Typically one vendor or another will agree to 45 to 60 days (or longer) terms on an open account basis. This is the same as a cash infusion for the business.

After a few months of satisfactory experience, the vendor will usually increase the credit authorization. And, as sales increase and the enterprise grows, selected suppliers should be given preference. It is advisable not to always pay vendors on a regular basis -- such as the first or end of the month -- since a prime vendor might develop an undue reliance on regular payments. Then, if the economy slows and payments are delayed, the vendor might panic, cut off credit, and demand payment in full, which could destroy the company.

14. Bank Selection

Open a checking and savings account for the Company in a local bank. Make a courtesy call to the Manager and outline your company policy -- that you intend to build the business from earnings and that any loans will be short-term during the first stage. Then, as the business grows, you will look forward to a more traditional borrowing relationship with the bank. Keep the banker supplied with annual financial statements. When warranted, request a modest line of credit, and borrow and repay several times annually.

15. Customer Base

In this manufacturing model, company policy is to market its products to warehousing (stocking) distributors nationwide, then worldwide. Prepare attractive two or four-color brochures and retail pricing sheets with good photographs. Contract with a local manufacturer's representative to introduce and field-test the product in the immediate geographical area. Pay the standard sales representative commission, usually 10 to 15 percent. Typically, the "sales rep" will begin with small trial orders which will increase as the product is market-verified and fulfills a need. In this interim arrangement, the Company is burdened with credit exposure for the many small accounts and resultant accounts receivable. After a year or two, the sales agent may agree to become the exclusive warehousing distributor for the area. If not, the Company may either select a warehousing distributor for the area, or sell direct to wholesalers.

Obtain a list of leading stocking distributors from national trade organizations (nearly every product is represented by such an organization), the *Thomas Register* at the local library, the Internet, and by phone calls to leading sales representatives in the areas which comprise the major market. Prepare an exclusive warehousing distributor contract requiring the distributor to place a substantial initial order.

Make use of extended discounts such as 35 percent - 15 percent - 10 percent (rather than 50 percent off retail list price) for the minimum order, and an extra 10 percent off for a larger order (55 percent off retail). Not only does the extended discount schedule appear more favorable to the distributor, it provides a ready pricing structure to the wholesaler and retailer.

Prepare a carefully worded cover letter addressed to CEOs, indicating that 'their company' has been selected as the leading distributor in the marketing area, and that signing and returning one copy of the contract, with the initial minimum stocking order, will constitute acceptance of the agreement. Sign the letter and two copies of the agreement. Include retail pricing sheets and technical information and, if appropriate, product samples. If there is one warehousing distributor servicing a given area, send one package. If there are two, three, or even four distributors in a major city, send a package to each of them. The first one to return a signed copy of the agreement with an initial order, all other things being equal, is granted the exclusive representation. Offer a liberal 'out' clause, authorizing either party to cancel the agreement with 30 days written notice. Enough orders should arrive from this low-cost marketing effort to 'jump-start' the company.

16. Utilization of Earnings

Use retained earnings for capital improvements, for reduced labor and material costs. In the second stage of company development, move into flex-space, combining main offices and production there. Register and file with appropriate agencies, and comply with all requisite social levies. The need for *deferred compliance* no longer exists. Using ICs may be discontinued or limited, and employees and a production manager may be hired. The entrepreneur(s) may now be paid a portion of deferred compensation. As sales increase and products diversify, a General Manager can be brought in to oversee operations.

The Full Commitment Entrepreneur

It is not unusual for entrepreneurs to begin a new venture without a day (or night) job or outside income to fund their living expenses. A reality check would indicate that the entrepreneurs cannot substantially reduce their existing daily living expenses. Therefore, in order to fulfill the beginning cash needs of the new venture -- if $100,000 in working capital is needed -- a substantial amount would also be needed to carry the owners' living expenses during the first year.

Typically, this type of entrepreneur does whatever is necessary to fund the enterprise: invests savings and all other available cash, takes out loans against life insurance, sells or encumbers assets, and 'maxes out' credit cards. If the real estate market is favorable, the entrepreneur may refinance the mortgage on the home -- or, if not, may obtain a private or institutional second mortgage. Family and friends are tapped for loans and/or purchase of equity in the new business. The new entity is organized in full compliance with governmental regulations. Employees are hired and payroll additions pro-vided for FICA, FUTA, SUTA, Workman's Compensation Insurance, etc., at a cost of thousands of dollars.

Hopefully, in spite of the heavy start-up load and the owner's need to live from initial capital contributions and first income, the new business will survive. However, too many new businesses fail because, instead of taking just a few months or a year, several years are required to get operations to a break-even level. In the interim, the entrepreneurs' expenses and the many and varied costs of compliance liter-ally *consume* the once adequate funds.

Where an entrepreneur commits only discretionary funds and resists debt, building an asset base primarily from profits and using *deferred compliance* techniques, the ultimate objectives for the venture may take longer to achieve, but the rewards may be even greater. The various stages of growth remain substantially the same in either scenario.

Growing the Product

There is the inventor-entrepreneur who may require 5 to 10 years to *grow* the product. This requires strong funding to support both the entrepreneur and product research. Financial gains from successful inventions are often swallowed up in the maw of the latest inventive dream of such driven individuals. The wife and family of the inventor-entrepreneur -- whose destiny is to grow landmark technologies -- are destined to sacrifice.

Example: My mother's niece married Philo T. Farnsworth, the true inventor-entrepreneur of television. Everything his family had -- or could get -- was constantly poured into his inventions. Then came his first breakthrough, in a whirling disc that resulted in the first television image. He went on to develop other new technologies, and his last charge up the entrepreneurial-inventor hill was to try to harness *fusion.*

The following is not a legal document but a suggested outline.

INDEPENDENT CONTRACTOR AGREEMENT

THIS AGREEMENT is between _____ hereinafter designated ("INDEPENDENT CONTRACTOR") and _____ (hereinafter designated "COMPANY").

WHEREAS: COMPANY wishes to contract with the INDEPENDENT CONTRACTOR for the performance of certain tasks and services;

WHEREAS, COMPANY'S place of business is located at _____ and,

WHEREAS, INDEPENDENT CONTRACTOR'S place of business is located at _____ ,

WHEREAS, INDEPENDENT CONTRACTOR declares that it is engaged in an independent business and has complied, is complying, and will comply with all federal, state and local laws and regulations regarding business permits and licenses of any kind required to carry out the said business and the tasks and services to be provided under this Agreement;

WHEREAS, in the event INDEPENDENT CONTRACTOR has assistants and/or employees, INDEPENDENT CONTRACTOR will be responsible for payroll or employment taxes to include, but not be limited to, FICA, FUTA, Federal income tax, State income tax, etc.;

WHEREAS, INDEPENDENT CONTRACTOR declares that it is engaged in the same or similar activities for other clients and that COMPANY is not the INDEPENDENT CONTRACTOR'S sole and only client or customer, INDEPENDENT CONTRACTOR hereby affirms that similar services are offered to the public.

WHEREAS, INDEPENDENT CONTRACTOR will allocate all the time and efforts necessary to accomplish the duties and responsibilities of this Agreement, it is understood that COMPANY will not regulate said hours.

THEREFORE, in consideration of the foregoing representations and the following terms and conditions, the parties agree:

1. SERVICES TO BE PERFORMED. COMPANY hereby engages The INDEPENDENT CONTRACTOR to perform certain tasks and/or services. The scope of these consulting services will include but not be limited to:

(a) _____

(b) _____

(c) _____

2. INDEPENDENT CONTRACTOR agrees to contract with other Independent Contractors/Subcontractors as might be needed to assure the achievement of mutually accepted goals, subject to the approval by COMPANY of same.

3. INDEPENDENT CONTRACTOR fees for services rendered, according to the terms and conditions set forth

herein are: payment by COMPANY against presentation of invoices for work performed.

4. INDEPENDENT CONTRACTOR shall submit invoices to COMPANY for services rendered at the end of each month during the life of this AGREEMENT.

5. INSTRUMENTALITIES. The INDEPENDENT CONTRACTOR shall supply all equipment, tools, materials, and supplies to accomplish the contracted and designated tasks and services; shall lease from the COMPANY, adequate space in which to perform the above and other services. If necessary, the INDEPENDENT CONTRACTOR will also lease additional machinery and equipment from COMPANY.

6. GENERAL SUPERVISION. The INDEPENDENT CONTRACTOR retains the sole right to control or direct the manner in which the services described herein are to be performed. Subject to the foregoing, COMPANY retains the right to inspect, to stop work at its sole discretion, to prescribe alterations and generally to supervise the work to insure its conformity with those tasks and services specified hereinabove.

7. NO PAYROLL OR EMPLOYMENT TAXES. No payroll or employment taxes of any kind shall be withheld or paid with respect to payments to the INDEPENDENT CONTRACTOR. The payroll or employment taxes that are the subject of this paragraph include but are not limited to FICA, FUTA, Federal and State income tax, etc. No Workman's Compensation insurance has been or will be obtained by COMPANY on account of the INDEPENDENT CONTRACTOR or INDEPENDENT CONTRACTOR employees.

8. INDEPENDENT CONTRACTOR will exert every possible effort to provide quality contract services, utilizing best efforts.

9. EFFECTIVE DATE AND TERMINATION. This agreement shall be effective _____ and end _____ and may not be terminated earlier (except for cause) without thirty (30) days prior written notice from one party to the other.

10. RENEWALS. This Agreement will be reviewed no later than 60 (sixty) days prior to the above date of termination, and if the performance of the INDEPENDENT CONTRACTOR is deemed to be satisfactory in the sole discretion of COMPANY, this Agreement will be renewed upon the same terms and conditions for an additional twelve (12) month period on the same terms and conditions. Subsequent renewals of this Agreement will be automatic for one calendar year each, unless either party notifies the other in writing, not less than sixty (60) days prior to date of termination, of that party's decision not to renew the Agreement.

	INDEPENDENT
COMPANY	CONTRACTOR
By_____	By_____

AGREED to this _____ day of _____ 199___.

IRS does not like the use of Independent Contractors.

I. The major IRS checks (triggers) are listed below, and should be carefully followed and reviewed periodically:

a) Neither the IC or his/her associates should be officers or key employees of the COMPANY, and should receive no compensation other than that of an IC.

b) IC hours of work cannot be regulated by the Company IC determines the how and when of the work;

c) It helps if the IC has an assistant or employee(s);

d) The IC should have own tools and equipment, or may lease machinery and equipment from the Company;

e) Repair on IC contract work should be paid by the IC;

f) The IC should have other customers;

g) Liability and health insurance should not be paid by the Company;

h) IC should pay own expenses;

i) IC should have office space or office help;

j) IC does not wear Company uniform with logos;

k) If the Company has the right to fire at will, the IC relationship would be in question;

l) The IC should have independent licenses;

m) If an IC advertises, it is a plus.

> "In the absence of clearly defined goals,
> we are forced to concentrate on activity
> and ultimately become enslaved by it."
> - *Charles Coonradt*

CHAPTER FOUR [

THE LEGAL AND TAX STRUCTURE

There are several legal structures available to the new venture: Sole Proprietorship, General Partnership (GP), Limited Partnership (LLP), Subchapter S Corporation (S-Corp), Standard C Corporation (C-Corp) with or without *1244 Election*, Limited Liability Company (LLC), and various types of Trusts. These structures vary from restrictive to flexible, with creative alternatives. Several are convertible to one or more of the other legal forms under certain circumstances, subject to specific restrictions. Others are closed-end, in that they cannot be easily be converted or transferred into another legal entity.

What might be the best legal form in the initial or start-up phase of the business may not necessarily be the most beneficial in subsequent stages of the enterprise. The entrepreneur should obtain information and recommendations in review with a qualified attorney and/or CPA. The following is a thumbnail sketch of each of these legal structure options.

Single Tax Entities

Sole Proprietor
This is basically the owner conducting business in his or her name or in a *dba (doing-business-as)* or *aka (also-known-*

as) fictitious name. The individual owner reports annual net income on the IRS 1040 personal income tax form for the taxable (usually calendar) year.

In general, the liabilities of the business are also personal liabilities, since the owner and the business are viewed as the same entity for tax purposes.

To begin doing business as a sole proprietor, it is necessary to obtain applicable occupational licenses (city, county and state), and to register a fictitious name, if used. *Advantages:* modest start-up expense and exemption from certain tax levies and payroll additions. Losses are deductible. *Disadvantages:* high direct and indirect liability exposure to the individual and difficulty in obtaining health and benefit plans.

General Partnership

Two or more individuals enter into a general partnership. The requirements of this single tax business form are essentially the same as those listed under the Sole Proprietorship. A fictitious name may be selected and registered with the state (*dba* or *aka*). The taxable period is usually the calendar year. Occupational licenses are required. *Advantages:* Partnership net income is taxed only once and flows through to the IRS 1040 personal tax form. Modest start-up expense and exemption from certain tax levies and payroll additions. Losses are deductible pro-rata to partnership interest. *Disadvantages:* High direct and indirect liability exposure to the individual partners, and difficulty in obtaining health and benefit plans.

Though a written agreement is not required by law, it is recommended that partners execute a partnership agreement prior to the initial *honeymoon* period. Basic areas of possible misunderstanding should be addressed, such as which partner will make the final business decisions in case of deadlock, the rights, duties and responsibilities of each individual, and a termination and exit clause. Partnerships don't always operate smoothly or, if they do, people or situations may change, so a buy-sell agreement is recommended. This is an offer made by one partner to buy the other partner's interest which, if not accepted within a reasonable period of time (30 days is often specified), requires that the offeree buy the first partner's interest on the same basis.

There is an inherent difficulty in maintaining a good working relationship. Partnerships tend to be strained if there are substantially higher profits than projected or, conversely, if the business suffers continuing losses.

In the former, the *greed button* often clicks on in one or both partners, leading to intense maneuvering to carve out a larger share. In the latter, family financial pressures may become intolerable and adversely affect the partnership (Susie cannot attend private school, etc.).

Limited Partnership

The Limited Partnership requires a formal written partnership agreement and filing of certificate of limited partnership with the state. There are statutory formalities. One or more general partners have the management responsibility, and liability extends to their personal assets. It is possible for a corporation to serve as the general partner, thus limiting individual liability.

Limited partners are not permitted to take active part in the management of the partnership. As a general rule, the limited partner's actual investment (plus appreciation) and commitments in the partnership agreement vis-a-vis future investment contributions, are subject to attack by business creditors, but not their personal assets. The Limited Partnership is governed by complex regulations and laws.

S Corporation

In the S Corporation, also known as the 'S-Corp' or *Subchapter S* Corporation, only one class of common voting stock is authorized, but the corporation may sell bonds. The number of shareholders cannot exceed 75. Annual net earnings or losses pass through to individual shareholders who enjoy limited liability in the corporation. Shares may be transferred, bought and sold. It is often beneficial to prepare a careful Shareholder Agreement with buy-sell and right-of-first-refusal provisions. Whether income is distributed or not, income tax is payable pro-rata to each stockholder's interest at the end of the fiscal year, which is usually the calendar year. Similarly, losses are deductible by shareholders.

For S Corporation election, all shareholders must sign IRS form 2553 on or before the 15th day of the 3rd month of the tax year. (By March 15th if a calendar year). Additional requirements are: Only individuals, estates and certain trusts may own S Corporation stock. Voting rights within the single authorized class of stock may vary, as provided in the By-Laws. Some shares, for example, may have no voting rights. An S-Corp may not own subsidiaries. S-Corp status may be terminated by more than 50 percent vote of the issued and outstanding shares. The corporation will then be taxed as a C-Corp. To reelect S-Corp status, a period of 5 years must have elapsed. Where heavy start-up losses are incurred, an S Corporation is a good choice because it permits losses to be personally deductible (pro-rata to ownership) by individual shareholders.

Limited Liability Company (LLC)

A relatively new legal structure is the Limited Liability Company (LLC). It is now available in almost all states. It is a non-incorporated single tax entity with the tax characteristics of a partnership, but with the limited liability of a corporation. There may be more owners than in an S-Corp, and any or all of them may be active in management.

There is a limitation on an owner's ability to withdraw from the company and it cannot qualify for Section 1244 ordinary loss provision. An LLC does not automatically qualify in every state for tax treatment as a partnership. In order not to be taxed as an association, the LLC should have limited life (30 years in some states), and not permit free transfer of ownership interests. Caution is recommended in selecting this form since there is little body of case law, nor is the federal tax status clear.

Trusts

Certain types of trusts are qualified to own businesses. Among these are 'standard' revocable or irrevocable trusts, and irrevocable complex trusts organized by private contractual agreement. In the latter, a Trust Indenture (Declaration of Trust) is prepared by the Grantor/Creator and assets are irrevocably conveyed to the Trust. Typically, the life of this trust is 25 years or more. Trustees are charged with protection of the Corpus (conveyed assets). Beneficiaries of the trust pay personal income taxes on distributions made at the discretion of the trustees and may not be active in trust management. Such trusts may be utilized together with private foundations. Federal reporting is on IRS 1041 and K-1 forms. In general, privacy is enhanced and the assets of the trust are less subject to business creditor liens or attacks. This type of trust requires detailed minute and record keeping. Due to income tax avoidance abuses in this area, the irrevocable complex trust system is under increasing scrutiny by IRS.

Double-Tax Entities

C Corporation

The standard 'C' Corporation is taxed on its net annual income. After-tax income, when distributed to shareholders as dividends, is also taxable. That makes this structure the prime *double-tax* vehicle, beloved by the IRS. Maximum corporate tax rates apply -- usually in the 34 to 38 percent range. Dividends are taxed as personal income. Alternate minimum tax (AMT) additions apply at certain income levels.

Several classes of stock may be authorized and a number of variations selected in a C-Corp, as long as they are provided for in the corporate By-Laws or in the amendments thereto. It is often beneficial to make a *1244 election*, i.e., qualify the C-Corp's stock as small business stock under Section 1244. Up to $50,000 of losses are recognized as ordinary losses, which are almost always deductible in full. This section was introduced by the provisions of the Omnibus Reconciliation Act of 1993, to induce investors to acquire stock in existing small businesses or start-up ventures. Non-corporate taxpayers may exclude up to 50 percent of the gain they realize on the sale of small business stock issued to them after August 10, 1993, and held for a minimum of 5 years. Total annual sales of the C-Corp may not exceed $50 million for this election to apply. Specific limitations govern the amount of the excluded gain and the qualifying trades or businesses.

The structure of the C-Corp lends itself to creative applications and various combinations of authorized stock. There can be Class A, Class B, Class C stock or Preferred Stock. Class A might be *organizer stock* issued to the creators of the Company at a nominal cost per share. Class B might be *investor stock* at the offering price per share. Class C could be non-voting, but income-participating stock, etc. There are almost infinite variations. For instance, Preferred Stock may be either a specific kind of voting stock, or a non-voting, non-equity participating stock with guaranteed rate of interest and redemption premium.

Advantages to C-Corp structuring include opportunities for *debt instruments with convertibility* into one or another class of stock (such as convertible debentures), loans with equity kickers, warrants, options, and other devices. Blocking rights, anti-dilution, non-assessable clauses, etc. are some of the protection devices against the *Bad Guys*.

Whatever the mix of classes of stock and their restrictions, they should be specified in detail in the corporate By-Laws and preferably in a carefully written Shareholder Agreement, executed by all shareholders with voting rights.

Again, it is important to use the services of competent certified accountants and attorneys in the organizational -- as well as the ongoing -- stages of the new business. Changes in federal, state and local tax laws may require annual review and perfecting, or even changing, the legal and tax structure of the new company.

The Nevada Corporation

For those selecting a C Corporation as their preferred legal structure, there are the traditional alternatives for incorporation: In the state in which the principal incorporator resides; in one of the handful of states which have no state income tax, such as Florida and Wyoming; in the ubiquitous Delaware corporation; or in the Nevada corporation. And, for some entities, offshore corporate registration may be an option.

Please note that the Nevada Secretary of State Office requires that there be a President, Secretary, Treasurer and one Director stated in the incorporating documents. There may be only one person in all the offices. Thus virtually any person could be elected President, Secretary and Treasurer. (It may be anecdotal, but in one case, a homeless person and in another a mother-in-law, were supposedly elected Presidents of such companies.)

In a Nevada Corporation, one or more Vice Presidents could be elected (yet not be disclosed), and be given all the powers and control normally reserved for the President of the corporation. This provides a high degree of personal protection and privacy. Another advantage is shareholder privacy. The incorporator is not required to submit a list of stockholders when filing for a new corporation, since Nevada requires no official list of corporate shareholders.

Liberal stock ownership is a fact of life. *Bearer stock* is authorized. It is also possible to operate multiple businesses within the same corporation. Another bonus is the fact that so far Nevada is reportedly the only state which has *no information sharing agreement* with the IRS. Any attorney embarking on a fishing expedition to identify assets in a Nevada corporation might find it a frustrating experience.

And, a word to the wise, there is a higher per capita IRS audit rate of Nevada corporations than in other states.

Other Legal Forms

The Family Limited Partnership

Application is made for a Family Limited Partnership by filing with IRS for a Federal Tax Identification number (EIN) using form IRS Form SS-4. One of many creative approaches to be considered.

Example: Mother and Dad, General Partners acquire 5 percent ownership each, the children as Limited Partners receive the remaining 90 percent. The Family Limited Partnership is a pass-through entity, and limited partners receive unearned income. Thus no FICA is due, resulting in savings as high as 15.3 percent on the applicable income. There is flexibility in the manner in which the Family Limited Partnership can be organized.

General Partners may provide that income not be distributed annually on a pro-rata basis to ownership of partnership interests, but held for future distribution. Of course, income taxes must be paid annually pro-rata to the childrens' interest in the limited partnership at their lower tax rate. This structure may permit savings in FICA and income taxes.

Note: There must be a bona fide business operation in the Family Limited Partnership or it may be disallowed by the IRS.

"Treat people as they are
and they will remain as
they are.
Treat people as they can
and should be,
and they will become as
they can and should be."
- *Goethe*

CHAPTER FIVE ▯

SQUEEZE UNTIL IT HURTS

New ventures are, more often than not, undercapitalized. This is especially true if the entrepreneurs have no outside source of income. They have no choice but to maintain an existing standard of living from capital contributions and/or loans. Another factor is that most new business projects take longer, and cost more, than originally projected. It is therefore critical that the owner-manager carefully identify and service only the basic needs of the business in order to maximize financial resources. Not a few entrepreneurs, in their optimism -- or for whatever other reason -- fail to husband available cash. Too often they confuse 'wants' with 'needs', a mistake which can be terminal to the budding business.

Management Tools

Cash flow, or lack of same, determines the health of the business. The entrepreneur must continually monitor and nurture the operation to assure a positive cash flow. Expenses and operating costs need be constantly evaluated and reduced, accounts receivable reviewed daily, their collection handled aggressively. Vendors should be urged to approve extended credit terms. These are tools toward a positive cash flow. It is important to set two immediate goals: First, to collect accounts receivable within 30 to 45 days and, second, to obtain 45 to 60 days (or more) credit from principal vendors.

Accounts Receivable Collections

Until company growth permits hiring an accounts receivable clerk, the entrepreneur must personally attend to the prompt collection of accounts receivable. Following is a time-tried method which has worked in my own and various client's companies. It is simple, yet effective. I have tried other methods with less success. The recommended steps are:

1. On a large 13- or 15-column lined bookkeeping sheet, prepare a spreadsheet for all outstanding accounts receivable.

2. Title the first column, "Name of Company, Person to Contact and Telephone Number."

3. Title the next columns in sequence, "Current", "30 days", "60 days", "90 days" and "90 days or more", (or "120 days", if preferred).

4. Title a space comprising several additional columns "Comments".

5. List and spread by date and number all outstanding invoices pending payment for each customer in the appropriate columns (30, 60, 90 or 90-plus days, etc.).

6. Total each column -- under step 5 above -- once all invoices are listed and spread by aging. It will be apparent at a glance where collection efforts need to be concentrated.

7. Use this worksheet as a master working document. Place it in a prominent place on the owner-manager's desk, easily accessible.

8. At the start of each business day, review past-due accounts -- oldest unpaid invoices first -- and call those customers. Patiently, but firmly, obtain a promise as to when payment might be expected.

   Under "Comments" (see 4 above), note the dates of customer payment commitments, possible rework and other pertinent comments.

9. As payments are received, pencil out invoices paid.

10. At the end of each month, prepare a new spreadsheet and continue the process.

11. Prepare and mail, at the end of each month, *a detailed* statement of account to each customer.

12. If the account is approaching 90 days past-due, a note similar to the following should be included:

    "Please advise if this statement is not correct according to your records. Unless we hear from you within 10 days, we will expect payment in full by _____ (specific date)."

13. And, finally -- follow up... follow up... *follow up!*

Advantageous Vendor Credit Terms

Often overlooked -- but important to the positive cash flow of the new entity -- is the value of extended credit from principal vendors. In today's vernacular, 'it doesn't take a rocket scientist' to understand that, if receivables are collected within 30 to 45 days of billing and vendors paid at 45 to 60 days, thousands of dollars of positive cash flow will be achieved. When principal vendors agree to approve extended credit terms, they become, in effect, short-term, interest-free lenders. When approaching the vendor, it is well to keep in mind that, due to their high mortality rate and the resultant collection hassles, the credit department has to exercise caution with start-ups. But, if there is a reasonable assurance of credit compliance, credit officers will usually authorize favorable credit terms -- mainly because they are also under constant pressure to enable their company to achieve higher sales and profits. The following process has worked for me and a number of my clients:

1. Meet personally with the vendor's credit officer (or other decision-maker). Review with him or her the Company's business plan, its projected profitability and growth prospects.

2. Project confidence and ability. Develop a climate of sincerity and trust. Remember, the credit officer wants your business, if the credit risk seems acceptable.

3. Emphasize that, as the vendor helps the fledgling new business with extended terms of credit, a *preferred prime vendor* relationship will be created which will continue as the company grows.

4. Request approval of a revolving credit line at 45, 60 or even a 90 days terms-of-payment schedule, depending on the indications of what the vendor might approve. Be prepared for objections such as, "We are not bankers." Acknowledge their concern and continue the presentation.

5. Be prepared for vendor approval of half or less of the requested revolving extended-terms credit limit on a trial basis. After a favorable payment history, over several purchase and payment cycles, the vendor will usually approve increases in the credit line. If one vendor declines to grant advantageous credit terms, contact its competitors.

Credit Ratings

Entrepreneurs are rightfully anxious about maintaining favorable credit ratings. Dun and Bradstreet is still the premier source of business credit rating, though with advent of the Internet and instant rating sources, this is changing. Good credit ratings are important to the new business. But knowledgeable vendor credit departments know the limitations of all rating systems.

By necessity, credit information published in D&B reports and/or on the Internet is not always current. It's not unknown for a business with good credit rating to deteriorate and even file for protection under federal bankruptcy laws between one report and the next. In order for the new business credit worthiness to be reported as correctly as possible, the entrepreneur should meet personally with the rating specialist of D&B and make sure the company's profile is accurately portrayed.

For a modest charge, usually under $100, a principal can order a credit report from several Internet credit reporting entities. If there are errors in the report, the reporting company is obliged, by law, to correct them. One of the most common errors is confusion over personal or company names.

It has been my experience that it is not necessarily a detriment to be rated 'slow-pay.' As noted previously, because my principal vendors authorized extended credit terms, all my new ventures were rated by D&B at one time or another, as "Slow pay, but always pays." Vendors continued to extend advantageous credit terms in spite of this qualifying comment. The "always pays" notation made the difference.

The entrepreneur should never, *and I repeat never,* personally sign on any vendor credit arrangement. Some vendor's credit people use the traditional banker's phrase when requesting a personal guarantee: "Don't you have confidence that your company will meet its obligations? If you do, why would you not guarantee the account personally?"

The entrepreneur's answer to the vendor is the same as it would be to the banker, "In all probability the Company will, in the future, require a number of additional investors, or even proceed to an IPO with public ownership. In that case, you cannot look to personal guarantees. With this in mind, our company policy is that officers do not personally guarantee vendor accounts. I would hope you have confidence that I (we) will see that payments are made on or before the date due, and that the account is handled in an orderly fashion."

A Word to the Wise

Sometimes it is better, even though less convenient, not to pay vendors on a regular basis such as the first, tenth day or the end of the month. Vendors tend to develop an undue reliance on regular, and especially, discount payments. Should the economy slow and payments of invoices be delayed, the vendor might panic, curtail credit and demand payment in full, which could destroy the company.

Example: In my corporate pre-entrepreneur days, I was General Manager of a manufacturing company in Puerto Rico owned by a man whose principal business was as a supplier of radar to U.S. Navy fighter-planes. While in a previous business, the Company owner's policy had been to take cash discounts of 2 percent-10 days, net 30 days in payment of vendor invoices. When his business cycled into a cash crunch, as most businesses tend to do, he informed the vendors that he would no longer discount invoices and pay at 10 days, but for a time would need to observe normal 30 days credit terms. Prime vendors, who had for years *counted on his payments to meet payroll*, panicked and forced the entrepreneur into federal bankruptcy protection rather than approve standard terms of credit.

He learned a valuable lesson and later became a millionaire many times over. His new policy was to pay vendor invoices on a random cycle, but rarely less than 60 days. And the radar company never again took a 1 or 2 percent cash discount at 10 or even 30 days on invoices.

Plant Auctions

I have often noted that the offices of many new companies, especially those owned by manufacturing entrepreneurs, are often small, indifferently furnished, even stark. They don't need -- or even want -- a better office. It's just not important. What *is* important is that available resources go to nourish the budding enterprise.

For the majority of entrepreneurs who prefer comfortable, workable and well-equipped space, it is possible to accomplish it within even the smallest budget. Every few months there are auctions of furniture, equipment, machinery and tools of defunct companies -- prematurely driven to federal bankruptcy protection by catering to 'wants'. Awaiting the auctioneer's hammer, are luxurious office furniture, expensive furnishings, like-new machinery, pallet racks, factory equipment, computers, etc. -- silent witnesses of former 'grand thinking'. These items can be acquired at a fraction of their original cost. Such auctions are advertised in local newspapers or by local auctioneers. It is advisable, however, to set a predetermined maximum bid level for *needed* items.

Cash Discounts

There are those who believe that authorizing cash discounts for early payment of sales invoices is a valid tool to increase positive cash-flow. In my entrepreneurial life this has been an illusion. Too often a cash discount such as, "2 percent/10 days/net 30" results in the customer continuing to pay at 30 days (or more) while still *taking the discount*. And, even when payment is received at 10 days, if the gross profit margin is less than projected -- as it often is in new ventures -- the 2 percent discount may cut into critical cash needs during the initial stage of the business.

As noted in the above discussion, failure to carefully and creatively use financial resources at the very beginnings of the venture, to *squeeze resources until it hurts*, will almost certainly lead to hardening of cash flow arteries. This is especially true if management is drawn -- for whatever reason -- to acquire *wants* instead of *needs*. This includes, but is not limited to, purchases or leases of more machinery and equipment than needed, expensive office furniture and furnishings, premature purchase of a building, excessive overhead burden, unnecessary emoluments, and ignoring or failing to fully-utilize the cash flow control tools described above.

Insights Into Planning

Within weeks, or at most months, after creation of the venture, it is important to create and work with a conservative business plan. This will include creating profit-and-loss and cash flow forecasts of operations for 1, 2 and 3 years. A 5-year plan is a good exercise, but may be a futile attempt to set parameters based upon present knowledge in a world of constant change, new technologies, new approaches, new markets, etc. Today's -- and even tomorrow's -- planned products or services may prove to be fragile niches, due to a host of unforeseen changes.

For more insight into planning for the new venture, there is a valuable reference, *The Game of Work*, now in its third edition (over 100,000 copies sold) by Chuck Coonradt. Years ago, I adopted as part of my personal creed, one of his maxims (he calls them 'corollaries'), many years before it appeared in the above-referenced book. This, and his measurement of work concepts, can be helpful to any entrepreneur.

> *"In the absence of clearly defined goals,*
> *we are forced to concentrate on activity*
> *and ultimately become enslaved by it."*

Selecting Professionals -- Their Roles

The Attorney

Once the preliminary business plan -- which is based upon conservative profit-and-loss and cash flow projections and with appropriate 'what-if' variables -- is in place, an attorney and an accountant should be consulted to determine the best legal structure and accounting method for the new business. The proposed company name is verified at the Secretary of State's Office (anyone can telephone this office to verify if the proposed name is available). Application forms are completed and sent to IRS to register the legal entity and obtain the Federal Tax Identification Number (EIN) from the Department of the Treasury.

The attorney consulted prior to and during the formation or organization of the business should probably become the company's ongoing legal representative. There are many advantages to developing a permanent relationship with a law firm consisting of specialists in business, taxes and labor law.

It is recommended that the owner negotiate fees at the first meetings with the attorneys for:

(1) The preparation and filing of Articles of Incorporation and Bylaws with the Secretary of State and organization of the legal entity selected, and

(2) To achieve the most favorable hourly rate for ongoing work. Typically the law firm will, in addition to forming the legal entity, be the Registered Agent, and prepare Minutes of the Organizational Meeting, First Shareholders' Meeting and the Board of Directors Meeting, Shareholder and/or Buy-Sell Agreements where applicable, etc.

Most states now require only an annual meeting of the Stakeholders and of the Board of Directors. A number of states authorize one director to constitute the entire Board of Directors of the Company, and authorize one person alone to be President, and to hold one or more additional offices. Boards of Trustees are usually required to have two trustees as a minimum.

Many owners prefer to prepare in-house minutes of the annual and other meetings of the Board of Directors and Shareholders of the company. Others opt for their attorneys to provide this service and retain the Minute Book.

The Accountant

In the start-up phase, any reputable accountant will suffice to do the bookkeeping and prepare monthly financial reports, as well as the audited year-end reports. As the business grows, an in-house bookkeeper will be needed. With further growth, an accountant and then a comptroller will be invaluable to the growing enterprise.

In the second and third phases of the business -- especially if the exit plan calls for capitalizing by the sale of the company or its assets -- it is often beneficial to contract the annual corporate reports to a local office of one of the major public accounting firms since:

(1) Prestige and credibility factors of such firms make it easier to obtain debt and/or equity financing in the later stages of the company's development.

(2) As the time arrives for implementation of the exit plan, prospective purchasers accept major national accounting generated financial statements more readily than local auditing firms, which may contribute to negotiating a better price for the Company and its assets.

(3) The cost for preparing the monthly and annual profit-and-loss and financial statements should not be much greater than such services by lesser-known accounting firms.

(4) Presentation of Financial and Operating Statements is usually (but not always) more detailed and professional in appearance.

In-house people should physically count and compute the annual physical inventory and limit the accounting firm's responsibilities -- and costs -- to verification of the inventory for the annual statements.

The Banker

Every new enterprise requires a banking relationship. Banks need to make loans. Knowledgeable bankers look for small companies with potential for successful growth, with a history of steady annual increases in volume of sales and earnings. As noted previously, rapid growth will inevitably result in the need for additional working capital, precisely because the Company is successful. With such growth, more working capital is required to carry accounts receivable, higher inventory levels, management and other needs. A good banking relationship can provide short-term cash needs.

Debt financing of a business is, at times, advantageous. But for the small to medium-sized enterprise, debt financing can be dangerous, as any stagnation of cash flow could spell disaster. The recommended policy for the average entrepreneur is to take on the lowest amount of short- and long-term debt possible in order to build the Company.

Notable exceptions to this policy are those of the entrepreneurial elite -- members of the so-called "Club of Terror." They make maximum use of debt to leverage their enterprises past the first, second and third stages, culminating in 'going public.'

At its worst, debt financing can be easily observed in the market, as large profitable companies take on substantial amounts of debt financing to merge or change ownership. Too often this causes them to stagger and dwindle under the resultant interest burden. Latin Americans have a saying that too much bank debt, *"es trabajar para el inglés"* ("is to work for the Englishman") -- an allusion to the business acumen of the British at the height of their Empire period, or, in other words, to make others work for nothing.

One of the first acts of the entrepreneur should be to identify a banking institution which understands the needs of the business, and then review its plan, strategy and prospects with the commercial loan officer, and discuss future loan possibilities. If satisfied, the entrepreneur should proceed to open an operating and, if necessary, payroll account. It is a fact, however, that bankers usually avoid making loans to start-ups unless solid collateral is available.

There is an anonymous story about an Indian who appeared at the local bank to request a loan.

"Do you have collateral?"

"What collateral?" came the response.

"Well, do you have horses? They would be collateral."

"Gottum plenty horses!"

And so the loan was approved and in due course the borrower appeared to repay the loan -- ahead of time.

"Me sell horses, plenty horses, for big money."

"Wonderful!" the officer said. "Would you like to put your money in the bank?"

The Indian looked at the banker, "Gottum horses?"

It has been said that your banker should think of you as a partner. This is true for businesses which rely heavily on debt financing to ramp-up rapidly to their IPO (Initial Public Offering).

I prefer to resort to bank financing only when absolutely necessary, since "The Goal" is to optimize earnings of the business to self-finance growth and build equity. I have also urged most of my clients to use institutional loans sparingly. My bankers, with rare exceptions, became friends, but were rarely part of my business life. I bought a commodity from them -- services and the use of their money for a time -- with the full knowledge that if anything went wrong, they could (and at times did) become *Bad Guys*.

Over the years, banking institutions have devised various types of commercial loan instruments, the majority geared to the short term, usually 5 years maximum. In addition to a traditional "2 for 1" (two dollars of asset value pledged for each dollar loaned) minimum collateral requirement, personal signatures of the principals of closely-held companies are a routine request.

Once a pattern of success and growth has been proven, a persuasive entrepreneur may be able to convince the banker to approve a *corporate loan*, i.e., a loan without collateral or the personal signatures of stakeholders. This is getting to be more and more difficult, however.

In my own companies, annual net profits largely met financial demands of growth so that outstanding loans rarely exceeded low-to-middle six figures. Company assets were never pledged, nor did I affix my signature to borrowings.

When the banker said...

"Why should we have confidence in your ability to pay, if you are not personally willing to guarantee the loan?" My response was...

"If you have confidence that I will see that the loan is repaid, why do you insist on my signature? Further, when my Company has additional stakeholders or 'goes public', personal signatures will not be possible, so why not start now?"

Example: Many years ago, I negotiated a revolving line of credit of $70,000 -- then a very substantial amount -- for my small building products manufacturing company from the local branch of Chase Manhattan Bank. No personal signature, no pledged assets. From time to time, the manager called to tell me that the bank might require my signature.

Two years went by. Then I received a large order for kitchen cabinets from a new Wherry Housing Project. I was able to increase the credit line to $150,000. That afternoon my

CPA called, anxiety in his voice.

"How did you do at the bank?"

"Fine," I said. "The credit limit was raised to $150,000."

He exclaimed, "I can't believe it! When I talked to the bank manager a week ago, he said he was not looking forward to meeting with you, because he'd need to have a personal signature or he would have to call the loan."

Another year elapsed and the banker asked me to meet with him.

"Gardner, the bank examiners were just here, and unless we have your personal guarantee on the loan they will classify it. I'm sorry."

"Frank," I replied, "How do you want it repaid?"

"$20,000 a month."

"Nope, can't pay more than $14,000."

He acknowledged that this was satisfactory, and I repaid the loan in less than 7 months from banner net profits.

Avoid Personal Guarantees and "Triggers"

In the first meetings with the loan officer enough questions need to be asked to determine the 'origination costs' of the loan or line of credit -- both published and hidden. Loan documents must be studied carefully for things like commitment fees, discounted interest in advance, lags in check clearances (the bank uses the client's money during 'check-clearing float time', and 'holds'), prepayment penalties, etc.

In addition, banks are fond of inserting 'triggers' or contingencies into loan documents, which place an undue burden on the owner in both capital cost and bookkeeping. Some of these contingencies are: A compensating balance requirement (a minimum amount of funds on deposit), no decrease in net worth, no decrease in working capital, failure to keep a certain debt-asset ratio, and many more. Any one of these triggers can automatically place the loan in default, subject to immediate call by the bank, *even though payments are being met on time and the loan serviced in a satisfactory manner.*

Make it clear in the first conversation that triggers are *unacceptable* -- a marvelous word for the use of entrepreneurs -- that the only acceptable contingencies in the loan documents are failure to make loan interest and principal payments in a timely fashion. If the banker insists on triggers, find another banking relationship.

Bankers refer, in their approval process, to certain ratios on financial statements, many of which are important control items for the entrepreneur. 'Inventory Turnover' refers to the number of times inventory is sold and replaced during the fiscal year. 'Accounts Receivable Collection Days' are calculated in a formula in which the total of Accounts Receivable is divided by sales, then multiplied by days in the period (usually one month). 'Receivable Turnover' equals Net Sales divided by average Accounts Receivable, etc. For an excellent reference on this subject, refer to Chapter 6 of *The Ernst & Young's Guide to Financing for Growth*, by Daniel R. Garner and published by John Wiley & Sons (1994).

Banking relationships with entrepreneurs are often ephemeral because of the mercurial nature of new businesses. An apparent cordial understanding, even friendship, with the banker, will all-too-quickly cool if the new business does not meet (for whatever reason) its projections. And, if worsening ratios appear on financial statements -- perhaps heralding temporary financial adversity -- the bank may, without warning, move from a position of support and financial backing to one of positioning to grab assets. Then the friendly banker' may become one of the *Bad Guys* with whom one has to be prepared to do battle.

Third Parties Can, and Do, Help

It is rare to find a beginning entrepreneur who has a full understanding of the basic elements of creating and growing a business. Most learn the necessary attributes of success through trial and error, sometimes at considerable cost. Too many are incapable of *listening* to counsel. My policy has always been to terminate consulting services, no matter how lucrative, if an entrepreneur or other client does not *listen* and follow recommendations. Such clients are described in a saying attributed to Benjamin Franklin:

> *"They that will not be counselled, cannot be helped. If you do not hear reason, she will rap you on the knuckles."*

Input from experienced third parties is a precious commodity. Two heads (or more) are nearly always more valuable than one, even if used only as a 'sounding board' by the entrepreneur. A number of options are available: A Board of Directors, a Board of Trustees (for a Trust), Advisor(s) to the Board of Directors or Trustees, Financial and Business Consultants, representatives of SCORE, COACHES, etc.

Boards of Directors

The Board of Directors of a corporation, whether a 'C-Corp', 'S-Corp' or 'LLC' may consist of one or more members in most states. The Annual Meeting of the Board of

Directors usually (but not always) immediately follows the Annual Meeting of the Shareholders.

Among the main agenda items of the Annual Shareholders' Meeting is to discuss matters of ownership, financial condition, business policy matters and operations, and to elect Director(s) for the following fiscal year.

The Board of Directors sets and implements policy under the direction of the Shareholders. It receives a report on operations for the previous fiscal year, and financial and other business reports from the President or General Manager. It also elects corporate Officers to serve for the next fiscal year.

A careful agenda for both of these Annual Meetings is important. Many companies also schedule Quarterly Meetings of the Board of Directors -- which are generally not required in most states -- at the end of each quarter and after financial and operating statements are available. Such meetings are excellent for management accountability and for detecting both opportunity and adversity at the earliest possible stages.

Many entrepreneurs, because of their independent nature and perceived need to make all the decisions in the company, are reluctant to empower a formal Board of Directors. This is understandable. It is also growing increasingly more difficult to find capable individuals willing to serve as members of a Board of Directors in today's litigious society. The personal exposure, even with expensive Directors' insurance, is considerable.

For instance, such insurance coverage does not prevent the endless days of discovery, depositions and court appearances which might befall a Director if sued as a codefendant with the Company. Also, directors are rarely compensated in small start-up companies. A better solution is to make use of 'Advisors' to the Board of Directors.

Advisors

As noted, Directors and Trustees face liabilities and are sometimes enjoined as parties to lawsuits brought against the business entity and its officers. *Directors' Insurance* is available to assuage financial exposure, but cannot eliminate court appearances and time-consuming legal procedures. One solution is to have no outside members of the Board of Directors or Trustees; instead use the services of Advisors who:

(a) Attend Shareholder and Board of Directors /Trustees Meetings, meet with the Owner periodically, in person and by telephone.

(b) Analyze Operating and Financial Statements, become familiar with policy, business plans, operations, etc. of the business.

(c) Provide guidance, counsel, market recommendations, financial and management input to the Owner.

(d) Advisors' names should *not* appear in Minutes of Board Meetings or official records of the business. It is unlikely that Advisors would be named as parties to adverse legal actions against the Company. There would be, after all, no paper trail, and testimony would have to be based on the Owner's and Advisor's best recollection of events and matters in question.

Boards of Trustees

Living Trusts, so-called A-B Trusts and Marital Trusts, revocable in nature, are usually not active in businesses, and are primarily designed to hold and protect assets of individuals and to avoid probate procedures at the death of a spouse. The rationale being that the trust is a continuing entity and survives the person's death. The Unified Tax Credit is applicable in determining the final inheritance tax assessable from the decedent's estate.

During the past year, however, largely unknown to the public, a state law was quietly passed in Florida calling for 'Administrative Review' of such trusts *similar to probate* and with a schedule of attorney fees. The only saving grace is that the wording states, "You may wish to engage an attorney." We don't wish to, but the filing requirements are onerous. In any event, such revocable Trusts are not operating entities and, for tax purposes, annual income taxes are reported on personal IRS 1040 forms. Trustees and Successor Trustees are designated by the Creator of the Trust.

For many decades the use of Irrevocable Complex Trusts) and Private Foundations (Charitable Trusts), was the domain of the wealthy few. For over 100 years these trust systems have functioned admirably (in the majority of cases) to provide distribution of tax-free private funds to nonprofit entities, usually pre-qualified under Section 501(3)(c) of the Internal Revenue Code.

In recent years, however, these Trust systems are being created at an ever-increasing rate. Unfortunately, some are formed by those who are *not* primarily service or philanthropy-oriented within the intent of the law governing such entities, but merely seek tax-avoidance.

In response, the IRS is increasing its attack on such trust abuses, targeting providers of training in the creation of such Trusts, as well as those who abuse the Trusts.

Tax forms for trust reporting are 1041 and 1041A. Distributions to Beneficiaries of the Trust are filed on K-1 forms and taxed at their personal tax rates. There are many types of Irrevocable Trusts. They may provide services such as marketing, management, etc.

In the case of the Private Foundation (Charitable Trust), beneficiaries are typically named as "all mankind". Most Trusts require two or more Trustees. There are many restrictions governing the selection of Trustees in this trust system. Trustees may not be the same individuals in the separate Trusts of the Irrevocable Complex Trust system -- and Trustees are even more difficult to find than Directors.

It should be noted that, contrary to representations of their promoters, such trusts are expensive to create and maintain, and especially to keep in compliance with IRS Codes and Regulations governing such systems. Unless the Grantor/Creator truly wishes to benefit all mankind, creating such a trust system might be hazardous to his or her financial health.

Business and Management Consultants

There are many entities and individuals specializing in consulting services to business. They operate basically on a fee-for-service structure. The entrepreneur should be cautious about consultants who offer to accept equity (part-ownership) in the Company in payment of their fees. A true consultant is fee-for-service and task-oriented.

How to identify the best consultant for the needs of the business? Most large public accounting firms have consulting services departments (often designated Management Services). Their people are usually well-qualified and the standard of service is excellent. Also, there are dozens of well-known large consulting firms in the market and a plethora of smaller sole proprietorships offering a wide array of services.

Unfortunately, since there are few state and no federal licensing requirements for Management Consultants (unlike Certified Public Accountants), almost anyone can become a 'Consultant'. Credentials are rightfully suspect. My son was once asked what my field of work was. When he replied that I was a consultant, the revealing question was, "What's the matter, can't he find an honest job?"

(a) Institute of Management Consultants (IMC),

This is a prestigious (but largely unknown) private non-profit certification organization, the Institute of Certified Management Consultants (IMC). The Certified Management Consultant (CMC) designation is individual and personal.*

(b) Elements of the Consulting Agreement

To evaluate a non-certified consultant, talk with previous clients as well as professionals who have had dealings with him or her. Once satisfied as to credentials, make certain that the body of the Consulting Agreement contains a full description of consulting services to be provided, and a 'cap'-- maximum total fee -- per task. Finally, insert a simple mutual 'out' clause whereby services can be terminated by either party upon 30 days notice (see sample Consulting Services Agreement at the end of this chapter).

Beware of consultants who 'open-end' their fees, or build from the task at hand to more and more services and fees. At least one of the so-called top consulting firms, whose first name rhymes with a generic alcoholic beverage, once had the reputation -- whether true or not -- of 'farming' the client for multiple ongoing services.

In spite of the above caveats, it is still a fact that knowl-edgeable business consultants can shorten the entrepreneurs' learning curve and accelerate profitability, and that a surpris-ingly large number of venturers use consultant services.

(c) *SCORE*

The SCORE Association (Service Corps of Retired Ex-ecutives) is a resource partner with the U. S. Small Business Administration, a voluntary organization of retired business persons who, at no cost, provide counsel and guidance to small companies. These volunteers are helpful, especially in the financial and management areas.

One of the previous limitations of SCORE, at least in our area, was that the person sent to counsel the small business was a retired senior executive of a large company, and usually had limited entrepreneurial experience. Whereas a new entre-preneur may have to do everything in the business in the initial stage, retired executives from large companies retain a corpo-rate mentality, and are accustomed to telling subordinates what to do. This mix of "doer" and "delegator" was sometimes frustrating.

In recent months, SCORE has shown remarkable entre-preneurial understanding by taking advantage of the Internet. Counsel is now available to any new business owner at no cost by logging on at *www.score.org*. The menu will ask for a brief outline of the business question to be asked. Then a list of executive members appears with background information on each. After scanning the list, one clicks on the counselor with the appropriate expertise.

My sample query to SCORE listed 64 executives. I selected a SCORE member from the list. This excellent resource will undoubtedly grow in the future.

COACHES**

"COACH" is not an acronym. A COACH is a valuable support system provided by an individual trained to give one-on-one guidance and support to the entrepreneur, following specialized techniques, as the name implies. COACHES work on a fee-for service basis.

(The following is not a legal document but a suggested outline only).

AGREEMENT FOR CONSULTING SERVICES

_____ hereinafter designated "COMPANY" is engaged in the business of _____, and _____ hereinafter designated "CONSULTANT", provides consulting and advisory services.

COMPANY wishes to engage the services of CONSULTANT and hereby enters into an AGREEMENT by which CONSULTANT will provide certain consulting services for COMPANY. CONSULTANT acknowledges having received $10.00 and other valuable considerations to enter into this AGREEMENT.

TERM OF AGREEMENT. This AGREEMENT will be effective _____ and remain in force for the period ending _____.

Notwithstanding the above, it is mutually understood and agreed that during the life of the AGREEMENT or possible renewal thereof, that either COMPANY or CONSULTANT may cancel this AGREEMENT upon a minimum of thirty (30) days written notice to the other party. In the event of such termination by either party, CONSULTANT will receive payment of fees for work performed to the date of termination.

SCOPE OF SERVICES. CONSULTANT will provide advisory and consulting services to COMPANY as follows:

(Example Only)

1. _____

2. _____

3. _____

4. To perform such other additional consulting and advisory services as may be required by COMPANY in writing from time to time.

5. IT IS UNDERSTOOD AND AGREED that CONSULT-ANT will devote best efforts to the good of COMPANY during the life of this AGREEMENT. For services provided, CONSULTANT is to be paid at the minimum rate of $ ____ per hour for a maximum of ____ hours, on a fee-for-service basis, payable monthly upon presentation of invoices. CONSULTANT will be reimbursed for out-of-pocket expenses such as travel, telephone and other ordinary business expenses.

6. COMPANY may from time to time request additional consulting services in writing from CONSULTANT, which will be based on the hourly rate noted above.

This AGREEMENT may be renewed on terms and conditions to be mutually agreed upon for an additional twelve months.

AGREED _____ COMPANY

AGREED _____ CONSULTANT

Date _____

*Notes

Institute of Management Consultants (IMC)

The original requirements to become a Certified Management Consultant have been relaxed somewhat over the years, but are still rigorous. Membership in the Institute when I was approved for membership, verged on being elitist.

An extensive *pre-application* form was required. In addition to questions of a personal nature, the applicant:

(1) Certified that he or she practised full-time management consulting for a minimum of 5 consecutive years prior to applying for membership,

(2) Was required to list and describe in detail the five most significant consulting projects during the previous 5-year period. These two questions weeded out all but qualified consulting professionals.

The candidate who survived the first 'cut' was then requested to complete a formal *application* as follows:

(1) Describe in detail the strategy, methodology, and level of success of each of the five projects recited in the pre-application form. If anything in this essay-narrative was suspect, the candidate was asked to clarify to the admissions committee in writing.

(2) After approval of the application, an intensive *oral examination* was scheduled before three peers, (in my case, two were from Big Five accounting firms, their Directors for Management Services; the third the owner of an independent consulting firm) -- a half-day event -- based on an in-depth review and analysis of the consulting projects noted above.

The process reminded me of an anecdote concerning a person who supposedly died and went to Heaven. Here and there were large groups of people playing and laughing.

The guide identified many of the leading religions. "Those are the Catholics, those the Methodists, those the Muslims..."

Then they came to a high wall. As they peeked over the wall they could see numerous people enjoying themselves just like all the other groups.

The celestial host whispered, "Those are the Mormons. They think they're the only ones up here."

IMC no longer thinks, "We're the only ones up there," but membership still connotes excellence. Merger with ACME, now AMCF (Association of Management Consultant Firms), has broadened their scope. There are, however, relatively few CMCs available in most areas, the exception being in large eastern cities.

And relatively few know who or what they are. It is somewhat disconcerting to have to explain to a prospective client what 'CMC' means.

COACHES**

WHAT IS COACHING?

There are numerous book references and dozens of web pages on the Internet profiling COACHES for entrepreneurs. The following is taken from several such references.

"Coaching began in the early 1990's mainly because many professionals started to experience an imbalance in their business and personal lives. Coaching is an ongoing relationship which focuses on helping the client, taking action toward the realization of visions, intentions, and desires.

"Coaching is a possible solution -- a positive and effective way to help individuals and professionals start their journey towards the road to achieving success and balance in their lives." A coach is your personal guide to help you:

- Discover what you really want.
- Develop a specific plan of action to get there.
- Remove obstacles over which you may trip.
- Resolve personal and professional problems.
- Integrate balance in personal and professional life.
- Recover from a major event or problem.
- Create a purposeful, focused vision.
- Free yourself from the limitations of the past.
- Find choices where none seem to exist.
- Progress in personal and spiritual alignment.

"Men who saw night coming down about them
could act as if they stood at the edge of dawn.."
- *Last letter of a Confederate Soldier*

CHAPTER SIX

GOOD GUYS AND BAD GUYS

There is an unwritten law in business that buyers and sellers must trust each other. The former count on receiving payment for goods and services provided. The latter rely on vendor performance.

Good Guys

A preponderance of players are "Good Guys". Some are Truly Good Guys -- honest, constant, supportive and loyal. Others are Good Guys under normal circumstances, but may become Bad Guys. A few Truly Good Guys I have known:

Illustration Capsule -- An Investor Good Guy
One of my clients owned a publishing business. Sales ramped up beyond expectations, straining available working capital. A private investor came forward. In addition to a substantial capital contribution, he pledged over $1 million in assets to secure bank loans for the company. The entrepreneur achieved initial success, only to fall prey to an ailment common to successful entrepreneurs -- a sense of infallibility.

The company expanded into other fields, which resulted ultimately in its filing for protection under federal bankruptcy laws. The investor could have become a Bad Guy and pressure the entrepreneur early-on to lower his exposure. Instead, he did all he could to help. His, as well as the entrepreneur's assets, were forfeited to service secured bank debt. To this day he is a staunch supporter and friend, a Truly Good Guy.

Illustration Capsule Two -- Another Investor Good Guy

My first venture was the leveraged buyout of a floundering custom furniture manufacturing company. My total personal assets were minimal so it was necessary to devise a creative proposal to acquire the business. I agreed:

(a) To loan the company $5,000 for working capital, (reducing my total liquid assets to $2,500).

(b) To purchase all the issued and outstanding corporate stock of the company with nothing down.

(c) That, shares of stock be held in escrow until fully paid, but with all voting rights assigned to me.

(d) To pay an agreed purchase price geared to a timeline of 1, 3 and 5 years. A base price would be paid during the first year. Or, if I opted to pay at a 3-year term, 25 percent would be added to the base price; if paid within 5 years, a 50 percent premium.

The business was reorganized, and new products were developed. My wife, Dorothy, stretched our limited personal budget masterfully, with no serious damage to our personal credit. The company soon became profitable. As sales increased, slowly at first, net profits provided sufficient working capital to service the increasing volume of business.

All of the annual profits could be used for this purpose because the company was income tax-free under the provisions of Operation Bootstrap of the Commonwealth of Puerto Rico. The NPBT (Net Profit Before Taxes) was therefore the same as NPAT (Net Profit After Taxes), which provided significant leverage.

By the end of the second year of operations, sales and profits had doubled. But earnings alone would no longer provide a positive cash flow. The corporate Balance Sheet did not yet justify a bank loan. Success was drying up the cash flow. At this point, entrepreneurs often bring in private investors in order to survive. This was not an acceptable alternative to me. It was time to be creative and not be *constrained by obvious realities*. There is always a solution. It is up to the entrepreneur to find it. As I reviewed the financial statements, a substantial liability stood out -- a loan obtained by the former owners from a private lender. Here was the key!

"Why not convince the lender to convert his loan from a debt to a capital asset, without diminishing my own equity?"

The following formula was devised, one which I have successfully used in several acquisitions, wherein private lenders exchange preferred stock for their notes payable:

> *Exchange existing short or long-term debt for preferred stock, fixed-dividend, with redemption-kicker (nonvoting and non-participating), redeemable at company option.*

In meeting with the noteholder, I said, "Hal, in order to save the company, I need bank financing. But present net worth won't suffice. Recently, you extended the promissory note which is much appreciated. I now propose that you exchange your note for preferred stock with a guaranteed annual dividend and redemption premium. This will be beneficial to you in better securing your debt, and will enable us to show the bank a much higher net worth, so that a working capital loan can be approved."

He didn't hesitate.

"Gardner, if it will help you, it's all right with me."

The net worth of the company was instantly doubled on the balance sheet. The corporate bank loan was approved. The company rolled forward. I negotiated final payment to the former owners and redeemed the Preferred Stock. A few years later, my exit plan matured and I sold the company for more than 25 times the original investment, income tax-free. This gave us additions to our 'gelt', as well as seed money to pursue another venture, largely because of a really Good Guy lender turned investor.

Illustration Capsule Three -- A Banker Good Guy

My second venture, the manufacture of mass-produced building products, soon required additional working capital to finance growth. The Manager of the Chase Manhattan Bank reviewed the loan application with me.

"Gardner, you are applying for a *corporate* loan. Why should the bank have confidence in you, if you do not want to sign a personal guarantee?"

I replied, "Frank, if the bank has confidence in my ability to pay, why would a personal signature be necessary? Also, when this becomes a widely-held private company or a public entity, you could not ask for personal signatures, so why start now?"

The corporate loan was approved, as were subsequent renewals, to more than double the original amount. When, years later, bank examiners threatened to "classify" the loan unless I signed personally, the Manager called me apologetically, "You either have to secure the line of credit with your personal signature, or it will have to be repaid."

I chose to repay the loan ahead of schedule. That banker was a Truly Good Guy.

Illustration Capsule Four -- Another Banker Good Guy

My client, a publicly-owned chain of fabrics stores, was over-extended. Two factors caused this. A free-wheeling CEO had paid too much *blue sky* (good will) to acquire competitors in order to ramp up to 196 stores serving the western "sew-it-yourself" market. In addition, the company had constructed a huge warehouse for distribution purposes.

The scenario was bleak. Three banks, including a lead bank, held $6.6 million in past-due loans. Textile mills, traditionally independent, refused to deliver fabrics, even C.O.D. As part of the restructuring, it was necessary to reestablish credibility with them, which we were able to do. Then we had to get the banks to extend the loans. Negotiations were successful and the principal banks agreed to roll-over $6 million. The remaining $600,000 was owed to a huge western bank. I did not anticipate any problem. To my dismay, the following conversation ensued with the loan officer of that bank:

"Mr. Russell, $600,000 is not a significant amount to our bank. I believe we can realize at least 25 percent of the loan if we call the past-due note now."

I leaned forward.

"Mr. Jones (not his real name) if you call the note, I will personally see that you get less than 10 cents on a dollar. Believe me, I know how. And, I will go on record to your superiors to that effect."

At that tense moment, another bank officer entered the room and asked my Bad Guy to do something for him. As he left the room, an impression came. I said to the new arrival, "You're a member of the Mormon church, aren't you?"

"Yes, I was born in Layton, Utah. I'm Vice President for Commercial Loans. Can I be of help?"

I explained the situation. He listened attentively and said,

"If the facts are as you say, I can see no reason why we cannot join the other banks. You have the extension. Don't mention it to Jones."

A week or so later, Jones called to tell me that he had gone 'all-out' to get the loan renewal for me. I thanked him profusely. I was saved from a Bad Guy Banker by a Good Guy Banker.

Bad Guys

Too many Good Guys become -- with slight provocation -- Bad Guys. They are Good Guys only as long as it suits them. They follow the rule of mutual trust while things are going well, because it would be detrimental to them to do otherwise. But, it is wise to be vigilant and prepared for apparent Good Guy investors, bankers, vendors, creditors and lenders to become Bad Guys.

The Investor Bad Guy

Private investors may be, by nature or by agenda, Bad Guys. Most private investors are Good Guys -- though the majority may become Bad Guys if their investments appear to be threatened. With this in mind, the wise entrepreneur will pre-qualify the potential investors. Here are a few thoughts which may be helpful.

(a) *Is the potential investor greedy?*

Greedy investors will stop at nothing to gobble up an entrepreneur's assets. They are the human equivalent of the cowbird which preempts another bird's nest, and pushes the nest owner's fledglings out to their death. Once a potential investor is identified as being, by nature, greedy, he or she should be turned away. Determining factors:

- Does the potential investor bad-mouth associates of previous ventures. If so, the same will happen to the entrepreneur, sooner or later.
- Contact previous associates of the potential investor and listen carefully to what they have to say.
- Assess whether the contemplated investor might literally stay awake at night to find ways to gain an advantage.
- Introduce the spouse to the potential investor and follow her intuitive feeling. He or she will almost always be right.

Greedy or potentially greedy investors are unacceptable and are inherently Bad Guys. Only if the situation is desperate should they be permitted to invest in the company. Then, all possible safeguards must be put in place during the 'honeymoon period'.

(b) *Is the potential investor a "Bump-and-Run" specialist?*

In Chapter One we discussed the phenomenon of the investor who offers to invest whatever amounts of capital are needed in exchange for a minority equity interest, then proceeds, over a period of time, to take over the company.

Unlike the greedy investor, B&R investors usually view

themselves as honest and fair in their business dealings, but they are Truly Bad Guys. They possess a large 'greed button'. They leave a trail of debris in the companies they have 'taken over', in the entrepreneurs who are no longer associated with the companies they created, or former owners who remain as titular employees with a minuscule stock interest.

If the entrepreneur is building a company for the long-term, the B&R investor should be avoided like the plague. Like the cowbird, this investor always succeeds.

(c) *Will the investor be relatively hassle-free?*

The most desirable investor for the initial phases of the new enterprise is one who has available discretionary funds, sort of 'throw-at-the-wall-to-see-what-sticks' monies. They view the investment as long-term, are supportive and helpful, and are willing to wait for asset appreciation.

Doctors and dentists, in general, do not fit the above profile and rarely make good investors in new ventures. If their investments do not provide a handsome return right away, or if the company fails to meet projections, they can become disenchanted, disruptive and/or threatening. At the very least they require endless hours of hand-holding and reassurance. Accustomed to relatively easy cash flow, they can easily become Bad Guys. There are, of course, exceptions. But, in more than one consulting assignment, I have had to make sure for my client that these professionals, once they became Investor Bad Guys, would Finish Last.

(d) *How to keep Investors from becoming Bad Guys.*

Provide each investor with informative monthly or quarterly operating and financial reports. Establish a personal relationship and maintain good communications. Avoid at all costs alienating minority shareholders. Attorneys have been known to advise clients not to be concerned about unhappy or dissident minority shareholders. Not so. I have verified from personal experience that a determined minority stockholder, in combination with a persistent lawyer, can cause an entrepreneur severe heartburn. Depositions and discoveries are the least of unpleasantries to be endured. Legal actions from disgruntled shareholders for fraud and/or mismanagement are not uncommon, and are difficult and expensive to defend.

Control of the venture in the initial stages is essential. This equates to ownership by the entrepreneur of a minimum of 51 percent of the issued and outstanding common voting stock, or other equity interest, depending on the legal structure.

Should investors press for more stock ownership, provide instead greater participation in company profits. One should not give up equity in the enterprise unless absolutely necessary. Keep control and management of the business.

(e) *The "50-50" Trap -- A Consultant's Dream.*

It is not uncommon for two individuals to start a new venture based on the fact that the skills and experience of each are complementary and basically of equal value. It seems logical to share equal ownership of the business. Not so. There are few exceptions to the following Premise:

> *Never enter into a "50 percent*
> *- 50 percent" business relationship.*

Experience indicates that equally-yoked associates may sooner or later (often sooner) become adversarial -- for whatever reason -- and reasons are legion. Differences and disagreements arise in how the business should be operated, or who has the ultimate say-so, etc. And, in not a few cases, the conflict arises between associates when their spouses disagree on trivial non-business matters.

As a result, a special shareholders' meeting is called in which one owner votes the 50 percent interest in favor of some matter of business, and the co-owner votes the other 50 percent against. The result is a tie, spelled *i-m-p-a-s-s-e*. The progress of the enterprise is stifled.

This is a consultant's dream. In the ensuing battle, one or both owners become Bad Guys. If I were involved, my client would, of course, be the Good Guy!

In an earlier chapter, there are suggestions on equity ownership variations to avoid creating Bad Guy co-owners.

The Banker Bad Guys

Knowledgeable entrepreneurs take precautions in relationships with banks, who quickly become Bad Guys when their rice bowl appears to be threatened. There are three main approaches in dealing with banking institutions:

(a) First, and most conservative, is to use bank loans solely for short-term cash flow needs, such as seasonal buildup of inventory, or to service increased sales. For this purpose, a revolving line of credit is probably the most satisfactory solution. Most banks prefer to see this type of credit 'zero-out' at least once a year.

(b) Second, use bank financing as ongoing working capital. Loans of from 3 to 5 years term, with a fixed repayment schedule.

(c) Third, leverage a modest capital investment with the largest borrowing possible, with repayment terms similar to (b) above.

Entrepreneurs tend to be optimistic, though they carefully assess risk. When preparing loan applications for bankers, three things should be kept in mind. First, will a conservatively-prepared financial statement be bankable? We have seen that there are creative ways of converting debt to capital. As Einstein put *it, "Imagination is better than intelligence."*

Nevertheless, entries of assets and liabilities should be realistic, not 'puffed up' to make the company's financial statement appear better than it is. Care should be taken not to overstate assets or understate liabilities. It is not generally known in the business world, but inflating a Balance Sheet to obtain a loan from a federally-insured bank is a *criminal violation* of federal law, even if the loan is not approved. In the case of profit-and-loss and cash flow projections for one or more years (in advance) and resultant projected financial statements, there is scant possibility of censure, since data is estimated.

Let us suppose that for whatever reason, the banker decides to close down company credit, thus becoming a Bad Guy. The entrepreneur in loan scenarios (a) and (b) above, must be able to determine (even if it's just a 'guesstimate') the maximum monthly or quarterly payment that can be generated to liquidate the loan on an orderly basis. This plan must be "sold" to the banker and, once approved, strictly followed. In the event conditions prevent meeting the agreed payment schedule, promptly notify the banker, and obtain permission for 'interest only' payments for a period, or even a 'moratorium' on loan payments for a specific period of time.

It is important that the bank understand that, unless there is flexibility and cooperation, the owner will not hesitate to terminate the company. As a consultant, I have offered to hand over company keys to more than one intransigent banker Bad Guy. Banks do not want failing businesses. Any repayment plan is better than a bad loan.

In the case of (c) above, the strategy can be different. Many high-flying entrepreneurs maximize institutional debt, so that, in reality, the bank loan is unsecured. Then, if there is a downturn in the business, the banker becomes an *unwilling partner* in the business and loan 'rollover' flexibility, workout plans, or refinancing arrangements are possible.

The Vendor Bad Guy

The vast majority of entrepreneurs has had the gut-wrenching experience of 'cash shorts' -- the inability to pay their vendors for a time. There will inevitably be the Bad Guy Vendor who will not accept a payout arrangement. The best defense is to send such vendors a minimal "good faith" payment every two or three weeks. Chances are they will accept the payments. This shows willingness by the Company to repay the debt and will frustrate, delay or blunt the Bad Guy's collection efforts.

Most vendors are Good Guys who will work with the owner. The following plan of action will work to keep vendors from becoming Bad Guys and initiating collection procedures when cash flow becomes tight:

(a) Immediately pay all past-due bills under $200, because these small debts generate inordinate dunning.

(b) Request -- in writing -- a detailed statement of account from all vendors.

(c) Reconcile the statement of account. Verify if there are credits due from the Vendor or possible claims for defective merchandise. And determine if inventory can be returned for credit with a 10 percent or even 20 percent restocking charge.

(d) Determine what can be allocated to Vendor payments each month and spread the available money more or less pro-rata (adjusted according to the vendor's ongoing value to your company).

(e) Send a letter to each Vendor in duplicate. Briefly explain the situation, and include the following paragraph proposing a minimum payout arrangement. Most will not sign and return a copy, but will feel bound by it.

"According to our records, we owe you a total of $_____. If this is not correct please advise. We propose to remit to you against this account a minimum of $_____ monthly starting _____ 19___. If this payment arrangement is acceptable to you, please sign and return one copy of this letter indicating your acceptance."

Should it become impossible to comply with the proposed payment plan, advise the creditor promptly and get approval for a new interim arrangement. *The most important thing is to keep the Vendor's financial officer informed.*

The Ultimate Bad Guy -- U.S. Internal Revenue Service

"Power tends to corrupt, and
absolute power corrupts absolutely."
-- *Lord Acton*

"The greater the power, the
more dangerous the abuse."
-- *Edmund Burke*

Never before in our history has so much power been granted, and/or unilaterally assumed, by any non-military government agency, as is the case with the Internal Revenue Service of the U.S. Department of the Treasury. The IRS has truly "swelled upon its agency" until -- in its unfettered power -- it literally dictates the economic life or death of thousands of Good Guys, i.e., the uninformed, optimistic or unwary entrepreneur.

The IRS has reached a new level of blatant arrogance in its willingness, even eagerness, to destroy people and entities in the exercise of its powers. I have observed their field people, agents and others, in what resembles a feeding frenzy. In our community, an IRS field agent was photographed by a local newspaper in a triumphant pose. She was holding aloft two cream pies -- one in each hand -- in the interior of a diner the IRS had just seized for nonpayment of Social Security taxes. She seemed to be saying. "These are my trophies!"

On the face of it, the display bordered on the ridiculous. But, the sobering fact was that she was enjoying her power to destroy a business.

Though many of its abuses have been subject to public scrutiny, and there has been a great deal of rhetoric about curbing its power, it is improbable that any meaningful restrictions will be placed upon the IRS by Congress. After all, the IRS is the source of the financial largess which gladdens the heart of the politician. It is, therefore, imperative to know how to keep this ultimate Bad Guy at bay. Here are a few guidelines:

- Never 'borrow' money from the IRS by failing to make Social Security or Withholding Tax deposits.
- The IRS is reluctant to agree to a schedule of payments on tax debt unless convinced there is either no "blood in the turnip" or that it would not be worth the effort to try to collect the full amount due.
- Assets may be placed out of reach of Bad Guys, including the IRS, *at the organization stage of the company*, as a matter of company policy -- but never once a claim is pending.
- If an IRS agent is intractable in an audit or workout situation, insist on meeting with the supervisor.
- IRS agents and other staff will assure the auditee that their hands are tied; that they cannot approve a 'workout' and schedule payments of a tax debt. Not so. They have broad authority to settle in the majority of cases.
- Never evidence anger, frustration or anxiety in dealing with IRS representatives. Be factual, firm and insistent, but never aggressive or confrontational.
- Answer questions concisely. Do not volunteer information. It might, and usually will, open new doors of inquiry.
- Have an accountant, legal counsel or consultant present if the IRS agent appears adversarial.
- IRS agents prefer anonymity. Learn all you can, as you would in dealing with any other professional, about the individual agent. But, be careful not to invade privacy.
- In the past few years, the IRS has developed armed SWAT teams who can, and do, descend on offices and/or homes and confiscate computers, files, etc.

without advance notice of any kind. Their justification is usually a letter from another government agency alleging wrongdoing.

- Try to be aware of possible IRS staff violations of their own applicable laws, rules, codes or regulations.

Many emerging entrepreneurs miscalculate their cash requirements and, when the cash flow dries up, they try to 'borrow' from the IRS by failing to make deposits for FICA (Social Security Taxes) and Federal Withholding Taxes of the firm's employees. This can be a terminal mistake.

Illustration Capsule One

A former client ('former' because he would not listen to my recommendations), a roofing contractor and an eternal optimist, *tripled* sales from one year to the next. He counted on net profits to service increased working capital needs. It didn't happen. The owner decided not to remit to the IRS either the employer or employee portion of FICA, or the Federal Withholding taxes. The resultant interest, penalties, fines, etc. were almost confiscatory over a period of time. Of the original $150,000 'borrowed from the IRS,' the company has paid the original face amount, but still owes nearly $200,000. Scheduled payments will not satisfy the debt for years. The IRS agent handling the case, in spite of company compliance, liened the business. The company struggles on.

Illustration Capsule Two

After many years of being owner or co-owner of income tax-exempt manufacturing companies in Puerto Rico, we relocated to Florida. My wife, who has handled all our financial affairs, also prepared our tax returns and endured various audits. For years I didn't even know where our bank accounts were. She still prepares a spreadsheet periodically to satisfy my desire to 'know-where-we-are.'

Upon transferring our assets to Florida, we were subject to an audit by the IRS. Dorothy met with the IRS agent several times and made two trips to Puerto Rico to obtain additional information to substantiate the basis we claimed. While yet on a third trip to the island to gather additional information requested by the IRS, a letter of assessment arrived. She was indignant.

"I will *not* meet with that agent again," she declared. I made an appointment with the IRS employee.

"Mr. Jones, I wanted to meet you, the first person who my wife refuses to meet with ever again. Now I can understand why. I would like an appointment with your supervisor."

He tried to convince me that I could not meet with his supervisor, to no avail. The supervisor -- a handsome, impressive woman -- arrived from Orlando the following week. She reviewed the documentation and asked, "Mr. Russell, is the basis you are claiming correct?"

"Yes, ma'am," I stated.

She turned to the agent. "Jones, wind this file up."

"But," he protested, "look at all this work I've done," holding up a thick file.

"That is your problem. Thank you Mr. Russell."

The agent ran some numbers on his calculator.

"Mr. Russell, we owe you $93," he smirked. "Don't hold your breath until you get it!"

"I won't." "Say, how do you like the (I named the car) you are driving?"

His face showed concern. He was no longer anonymous.

I smiled. "I like to know as much as I can about you, in the unlikely event our paths cross in the future, because you have acted like a real jerk."

Illustration Capsule Three

My client, a manufacturer of electronic equipment, asked me to meet with the IRS auditor. The agent was arrogant and adamant. I stood, carefully closed my briefcase, and turned to leave.

"Why, where are you going?"

"You apparently do not wish to settle this case, so I see no need to discuss it further."

In a more conciliatory tone, he asked me to sit down. In the conversation which ensued, I asked how his wife's swimming pool supply business was doing. He was surprised that I knew of their outside business interests. By piercing his anonymity, the atmosphere of our meeting changed. We came to an agreement on a reasonable workout plan for my client.

IRS agents are only human. By lifting the cloak of anonymity, most will be more inclined to be flexible. For less than $100. credit-reporting agencies will provide considerable information about anyone, which might be helpful in advance of a meeting with the assigned IRS agent. Perceived anonymity makes the agent aggressive, at times arrogant. Piercing it in a non-threatening or friendly "get-acquainted" manner will get his or her attention. State that it is company policy to obtain background information on any new business contact.

Illustration Capsule Four

Another client owned a growing womens' handbag leasing company. The essence of the business was to supply inventory in the leading department stores, with each item pre-ticketed. As the clerk sold a handbag, a portion of the ticket was torn off and placed in the cash drawer. At the end of each week, the store paid the total sales ticket amounts, less 25 percent, and inventory was resupplied. It was a good business opportunity for a beginning entrepreneur.

Unfortunately, the owner lacked an understanding of the importance of cash flow, and spent cash receipts as they were collected. He insisted that his daughter be educated in an expensive private school. Added to his misfortunes, his wife had been in a psychiatric clinic for several months. He filed the appropriate tax returns, but could not pay the federal income taxes. An IRS agent telephoned and talked to the wife.

"Unless we receive payment of the taxes owing we will lien your home!"

She, understandably, was very upset, since she knew nothing about her husband's business. I met with the IRS agent and showed him a power of attorney.

"Mr. Smith, the owner of XYZ Company has authorized me to negotiate a schedule of monthly payments of the tax debt."

"Mr. Russell, the only solution is payment in full at this time."

"We have a challenge, Mr. Smith. You are familiar with a Federal Act, supported by IRS regulations, that if you, as an employee of IRS, divulge information to unauthorized persons, you will be subject to a minimum personal fine of $1,000?"

He nodded in the affirmative. I had his full attention.

"You telephoned the wife of the owner of the business, and told her that, if the taxes were not paid, you would lien their home. Apparently you did not know that she had been undergoing psychiatric treatment due to mental illness. Her doctors had given strict instructions to the husband to keep her from knowing about the problems of the business. Your telephoned threat caused her considerable distress and possible hospitalization. She is not a shareholder, and indeed knows nothing about the business."

I assured the IRS agent that my client was not going to file a complaint, but he had to have a payment schedule he could live with. The total owed was in low-to-middle five figures.

"Mr. Russell, what do you propose?"

"He can pay, until things improve, $2,000."

"Per month?"

"No, annually, until he can increase the payments."

"Per year..."

He paused, realized there were no resources to accelerate collection, and agreed. We then talked amicably about a mutual friend with whom he had played football in college.

My negotiations with the IRS in behalf of clients have been infrequent, but I always establish and keep good ongoing relations with their people.

Illustration Capsule Five

Approximately two years ago, a leading tax preparer in Hawaii, whose seminar I once attended, told me that she was awakened in her home at midnight by a SWAT team of six armed IRS agents, all reportedly of Japanese-American descent. They forced their way into the home and stood by her bed with guns drawn. They carried off her computers, all files and records of her several hundred clients. Apparently, they justified the break-in by a letter from another government agency, alleging that she might be in violation of the famous (or infamous, as it is now being applied) RICO Act.

She prevailed in two court actions brought by the IRS and set about to rebuild her practise. To her surprise, nearly a year later, local authorities were provided with adverse information apparently gleaned from her computer files. After an accelerated criminal trial, she was convicted and is now in a California federal prison, pending appeal. Her business was destroyed and one of her staff also convicted and imprisoned. Great care must be exercised not to violate any federal law. Not knowing is, of course, no excuse.

Illustration Capsule Six

Not too many months later, the owners of a business for which I had provided limited consulting services (they *really* didn't listen), informed me that 12 members of an IRS strike force entered their home (the office was at their home) early one morning with guns drawn, and took computers, files and records. During the attack, one of the agents who stood by the bathroom door, heard it open, whirled around and aimed his revolver at the head of the couple's 5-year old son, who had been attending to his early morning needs.

During the raid, the leader of the SWAT team told the owners that they must have offended someone important (in the IRS) since the team had been scheduled for 'another hit,' but, at the last moment, had been diverted.

The IRS can and will obtain sufficient authority from other government agencies, if they consider it sufficiently important, to impound corporate and personal files by force, and without notice.

Fortunately, most entrepreneurs will not face the prospects of an official home invasion by the IRS. However, incidents like these should make it abundantly clear of the necessity of not keeping sensitive business documents on the business premises, in any event.

A Pound of Prevention

For those who "push the envelope" (admittedly a minority) and might feel threatened by the possibility of such IRS invasions, there are a few creative and admittedly heroic measures to keep this Bad Guy at bay, or at least slow it down:

- Sell all company and personal computers, hard drives, disks, etc., to a third party. Lease them back under a valid lease agreement. Affix labels to each item clearly indicating their ownership. The *IRS might be reluctant to confiscate property owned by others.*

- Avoid working with or storing sensitive information on company computer hard drives or discs in the office. Work on *borrowed* tape or Iomega ™ *Jaz* and *Zip* drives, *owned by the company's attorney,* that will hold all the confidential contents of the office computer. Return these computer drives to your attorney periodically so they are never truly in your possession. The IRS would find it very difficult to get hold of them because of *attorney-client privilege.*

- Enter into an agreement with the corporate attorney to engage, on the Company's behalf, outside accountants and/or CPAs and pay for their services on behalf of the firm. The attorney will then bill the Company for the legal (accounting) services rendered, as well as an incentive handling fee. *Attorney-client privilege.* The attorney will not permit the IRS to access accounting or other financial records.

- Purge all on-site computer files, corporate records etc., which might be used against the taxpayer. Keep office and personal files as clean as the proverbial whistle.
- If things do not go well in meetings with the agent or auditor, ask for the Supervisor. Auditors are taught to rule gray areas in the IRS's favor. Supervisors are taught to rule gray areas in favor of the taxpayer, and have a greater knowledge of the tax law and its application than auditors or agents. Some supervisors will stand behind their agents, but it doesn't hurt to try.

Additional Notes.

There are a number of publications which provide guidance if the entrepreneur is audited. Thumbnail excerpts:

"It's important to mind your manners when you're being audited. Contrary to what many people believe, you can be aggressive and well-mannered at the same time. Here are rules to follow:

- Say little; smile a lot. *Never* volunteer information.
- If you feel strongly about your position, let the auditor know. Often the auditor will let the point go in your favor.
- Provide as much documentation as possible for each point in an audit.
- Don't give up, even if you don't have all the documentation.

- Don't make too many concessions.
- Don't be rushed unless you feel hurrying will work in your favor.
- Don't complain about the tax system -- the IRS auditor pays taxes, too.
- Don't take your crumpled up receipts in a brown paper bag. That old strategy won't work anymore. Auditors are trained to believe that if you keep records in a disorganized manner, there must be an error in there somewhere.
- Don't take the Fifth Amendment. Tax protesting is a disaster. The jails and courts are full of people who believed such nonsense would work.
- Don't try to tape-record the conversation. The IRS found from experience that recording tended to fluster auditors. Recording was once a great way to get control of an audit, but now, you'll have to go to court to get permission to record. Even if you win, it's not worth the trouble.
- Act with confidence you're right. You probably are."

CHAPTER SEVEN ▯

HOW TO MAKE BAD GUYS FINISH LAST

We have noted that eldest sons and daughters of entrepreneurial fathers and/or grandfathers (some times skipping a generation) follow in their footsteps. If the predecessor was relatively cautious, stayed free of debt, built the enterprise carefully, conservatively, to create asset value, with a view to capitalizing, the progeny often renews the cycle.

Like their ancestors, they have a built-in impatience to move-on to new endeavors and leave the growing and polishing of the business to professional managers.

Studies show that, by age 55, creator-innovators originate five different ventures, on the average. Apparently, the energies, enthusiasm and dedication which are the mark of 'young Turk' innovators, flag considerably by then. There are of course, exceptions. I have met indefatigable septuagenarians fully involved in creating more than double that number of entities.

As for myself, I have completed my allotted five ventures (and more) from inception to capitalization. I am still open to new opportunities, but only if they meet my criteria:

- No more than three employees.
- Semi-automatic or automatic molded or manufactured subassemblies.

- Straightforward final assembly of products designed for sale to stocking distributors.
- Net profits of at least 15 percent of sales.

The Exit Plan

Premise: In the absence of a valid exit strategy, events will inexorably dictate the final exit plan for the business.

One characteristic of entrepreneurs is that they almost always have a valid exit plan -- selected in the initial planning stage -- which reflects the creator's purpose, needs, beliefs, background and persona.

Exit plans may be as varied as each venturer's needs and purposes. In the absence of an Exit Plan, it is probable that an involuntary exit will be enforced by any of a number of circumstances: loss of market, competition, a better mouse-trap, changes in customer acceptance, inept management, catering to wants instead of needs, lack of cost controls, etc.

It is a proven fact that only a small percentage of businesses survive the first year of operations. Many more fall out -- unless able to adjust the mix of products and services to changing markets -- during the first 5 years, dubbed the 'half-life' of a business. A minority of companies continue in a growth pattern beyond 10 years. I recently noted from a printed program, announcing a worldwide church conference in 1932, that less than 10 percent of local advertisers survived.

Entrepreneurial ventures fare considerably better than the norm because, in general, they are founded on more careful analysis and research as to market niche, viability of product or services, etc. All possible risk is usually eliminated in the start-up phase. As previously stated, entrepreneurs are not risk-takers.

Three reasons for selecting a voluntary exit plan :

1. *Capitalizing.* A date is set for the future sale of the legal entity or its assets based upon achieving a predetermined level of sales and earnings that would permit capitalizing at a selling price of five to eight times annual earnings, averaged over the preceding 3 years.

2. *Sweat Equity.* Similar to (1) above, is owners' deferred compensation, which minimizes the costs of administration, plus *deferred compliance* with social levies. There is minimal institutional debt, resulting in a higher level of annual profits, so that the multiplier should result in a higher selling price for the stock or assets, and a higher return on investment (ROI).
   Even though the Buyer adjusts the offering price downward for the amount management should have been paid, the Seller will enjoy the highest ROI possible. A possible disadvantage: That, using this bare-bones approach, the optimum time for sale might be delayed.

3. *To Build Gelt*.* Gelt is the formation of capital sufficient to provide flexibility to its creator. It is not to be touched for investment in new or existing ventures. It takes many forms, from diamonds hidden in the hollowed-out heel of a desperate refugee's shoe (their survival gelt) to sufficient resources for life's emergencies and/or to keep its creator from outliving his or her income. (* See page 166)

Gelt is also a vehicle to enable an individual to live a life of service to God, church, family and community. Dorothy and I accumulated our gelt in order to be ready for any unpaid volunteer 'calling' in our church. For me, though my ventures were exciting, business was not the *all-in-all* but a vehicle to accomplish my dream of service. It has enabled us to serve as full-time volunteers for more than two decades in foreign countries. Gelt-acquisition provides a financial safety net, flexibility, and a means for individuals to follow their true dreams.

It is important for the entrepreneur, at the outset, to analyze the mission and purpose of the venture and determine, in advance, a satisfactory Exit Plan and work toward it. Decide whether the goal is to capitalize, to achieve gelt, or to grow the business for the benefit of self, family members, etc.

Five Basic Types of Exit Plans

1. *Exit by IPO.* Hard-driving men and women typically organize a new business and ramp it up from stage to stage, culminating in an Initial Public Offering (IPO). Though they may maintain a minority position in the public company, their main thrust is to create a new company with capital acquired from an IPO, and move it along the same path as the first venture. They may do this again and again. Some speak of a life of terror because of the inherent pressures and personal financial exposure along the way.

2. *Building Block Exit.* Others envision their Exit Plan as one of ongoing 'building block' activity, broadening -- through acquisition and innovation -- new and complementary markets. They often seek financing in the public market. Bill Gates and Microsoft are the most visible leaders of this strategy. Their plan to exit is through control of new markets and accelerated growth.

3. *Exit by Succession.* Still others continue to expand the company into new products and services, adjusting marketing strategies along the way. The Exit Plan is one of succession, the transfer of control from father to son. J. Willard Marriott and his humble beginnings with one Hot Shoppe is one example.
   Another example is a former client who owns a company which provides purchasing services for hospitals. Sales have reached one billion dollars annually. He and his sons and daughters are the sole owners. It is not unusual for closely-held private companies to be grown into high-volume continuing enterprises.

4. *Exit by Capitalizing.* The majority of entrepreneurships involve the creation of specific products or services, exploiting a market niche into small or medium-sized ventures. There are two basic profiles:

(a) Those entrepreneurs who quit their 'day jobs' to devote full-time to the new business, and have no choice but to support their basic standard of living from their resources and borrowed capital. They typically mortgage their homes to the hilt, cajole family and friends for loans, aggressively seek investors, etc. As the business grows, interim bank financing is used. Rarely do these enterprises attract the attention of venture capital sources, nor do they 'go public' with an IPO. If the project fails, the resultant debris is awesome. If it succeeds all the players may benefit.

(b) Those who initiate the new venture with minimal personal capital. They rely on income from employment, fees, or other sources to meet their family's monthly expenses. They rarely accept loans from others, and take nothing -- often not even reimbursable expenses -- out of the company in the first or second stage of growth. With minimal administrative costs, they are able to build the business rapidly with far less capital. This is the domain of sweat equity.

5. *Exit Through Strategy.* Business owners in need of capital to build the company for the long-pull, should, as was noted in previous chapters, avoid the Bump-and-Run investors. B&R people are creator/implementers for their own kind of Involuntary Exit Plan.

But there is an exception. The Bump-and-Run investor can be beneficial to the entrepreneur who plans an orderly exit to capitalize. Why? Because the goal of both parties is the same. That is, for the entrepreneur's interest to pass to the investor. It then becomes a matter of *when* that takes place and *for how much.* There are ways to make such Bad Guy investors become Good

Guys in spite of themselves. Because of their nearly 100 percent success rate in lucrative takeovers, B&R investors tend to believe they are infallible. Therefore, it is possible for the owner of the targeted enterprise to insist on three main non-negotiable items as part of the initial funding agreement:

(a) The owner of 100 percent of the common voting stock in Newco agrees to sell a minority interest to the investor. As a *non-negotiable* item, the entrepreneur insists that 25 percent of the capital voting stock of the company owned by him or her be *fully-paid and non-assessable*. That stock can never be assessed for additional capital or subject to any call for additional funds.

The remaining 75 percent is assessable, pro-rata to ownership, and subject to 'calls' for additional capital pro-rata. In the discussion, the owner should quietly but firmly state that a percentage of ownership must not be assessable or subject to dilution. Anything less would be "unacceptable".

Example: Let's suppose that the B&R investor acquires 40 percent ownership for the initial capital infusion. The entrepreneur then owns 60 percent of the issued and outstanding voting common stock of the company (applicable to an 'S' or 'C' Corporation). When additional capital is required on the 'first go-round,' the owner-creator must fund, pro-rata, the 35 percent stock still assessable.

If unable to meet the pro-rata assessment, the worst scenario is that the owner's assessable percentage of ownership will be diluted. But, as the investor acquires additional shares for substantial sums paid-in, the original 25 percent, being fully paid and non-assessable, becomes considerably more valuable. The human cowbird is forced to feed the true owner.

(b) The second non-negotiable requirement is to include language in the Agreement that it is *unacceptable* -- a wonderfully effective word -- to sign personally on any company obligations. And, of course, this applies to the spouse as well.

(c) The third non-negotiable element of the Agreement is that Shareholder and Buy/Sell Agreements, advantageous to the entrepreneur, be executed at the same time as the Investment Agreement. Clauses to be included are:
   - Right of first refusal. If a bona fide offer is received from third parties for the stock of either investor, the other shareholder(s) will have 30 days to purchase the stock on equal terms and conditions.
   - Buy or Sell. If one investor refuses a written offer to purchase his or her shares, that investor must purchase the offeror's shares on the same terms and conditions.
   - Insert a clause to the effect that the Right of First Refusal, or the Buy or Sell will not apply to any investor whose stock ownership percentage is less than 10 percent.

How to Make Bad Guy Investors Finish Last

The optimum solution for any entrepreneur is to provide start-up and working capital through self-generated seed capital (savings, investments, etc.) and loans to the company by family and friends or shares of stock purchased by them. Should this prove to be inadequate for ongoing company needs, additional equity or debt funding from third parties becomes a necessity.

The process to pre-qualify an investor was outlined in a previous chapter. If, however, the investor selection was faulty, or the investor changed from Good to Bad Guy, it is possible to make that Bad Guy Finish Last. *From my experience I have found that there is always a way to solve the Good Guy's challenges. It is a matter of being creative, resourceful, and bold. But, each case is different.*

Illustration Capsule One

Scenario: Not too long ago, a client approached me to try to settle pending litigation. For health reasons, he had sold the stock of his thriving company, which contracted purchasing services to hospitals, nursing homes, restaurants, etc. for an initial down payment and a schedule of quarterly payments. Somehow in his subsequent move to another state, all purchase documents and files disappeared. The tough-minded buyer, a Bad Guy street-fighter type, found an excuse to cease making payments.

Prior to engaging my services, the client had sued for specific performance and was almost immediately served with a counter-suit in high five figures. Attorneys were positioned to do battle, fee clocks had started to run.

As I reviewed the situation, it was obvious that my client might not prevail because there was no paper trail. I called the Buyer, who at first referred me to his attorney. My suggestion was that it might be beneficial for him to listen unless he enjoyed paying legal fees. We entered into direct negotiations which proved fruitless, because the Buyer was not motivated. I decided it was time to get his attention.

"Mr. Jones (not his real name), I am sorry we could not work something out, because that means there will have to be a struggle. And I want you to know that I never lose a struggle."

It is important not to use the word "fight" since it invites confrontation. "Struggle" does not. Sometimes the entrepreneur must have some of the attributes of the little yellow dog, in the story below, to make Bad Guy Investors Finish Last.

A beautiful young lady walked her Great Dane every morning. One morning a small Latin man came toward her with an ugly little yellow dog on its leash. She asked, "What breed of dog is that?"

"Before I tall you, don' use zee word (he spelled it out) 'f-i-g-h-t', or me dog, hee keel yours."

"You mean that if I say 'fight' your dog will attack mine?"

In an instant the little dog jumped up and with one bite, killed the Great Dane.

"My, what kind of dog is that?"

"Before zey cot off hees tail and paint heem yallow, zey call heem 'crocodile.'" (author unknown)

"Mike (by now we were on a first name basis), you are aware of the Shareholder Agreement which governs the Company's stakeholder interests. You have issued to yourself a large number of shares of the common voting stock of the Company and have diluted my client's interest."

"Yes, I know," he said.

"And, by doing so, you also diluted a third party minority shareholder to the point where she now owns less than 10 percent of the issued and outstanding shares. Therefore, she is excluded from the restriction in the Buy/Sell agreement which states that "Owners of less than 10 percent of the shares of the Company are not bound by the Agreement."

"What's your point?"

"Well, what would you say if I told you that I met with her and found her to be very upset at the dilution. And let's suppose she has agreed to sell her shares to your competitor, who appears anxious to own minority shareholder rights in your Company."

There was silence for a long moment.

"What do you propose?"

"That you pay my client a lump sum of (and I named the amount), that all litigation be dropped, and mutual releases signed."

We negotiated a final amount and the matter was settled.

A few months later he telephoned me, "Gardner, I need your help with a problem..."

Illustration Capsule Two

Scenario: My third entrepreneurial project was the creation of an investment company, sort of a mini-venture capital entity. In addition to my paid-in stock interest, I was to receive a modest salary. My associate, a private lender, was to provide short- and long-term loans. The purpose of the business was to create new manufacturing companies and acquire equity interests -- minority or majority -- in existing troubled tax-exempt manufacturing companies and to provide funding and management. The exit plan was to grow each company and capitalize by selling assets or equity.

Within a few months we had organized a start-up plastics company and acquired a failing fiber broom factory. Due to an unexpected downturn in my associate's main business, he could not supply the promised funding. My gelt was intact, and I intended that it remain so. There was no choice but to seek out additional investors.

A youngish, sun-bronzed man named Sam came to see me, referred as a potential investor. He had recently inherited several million dollars. He had sailed his yacht to Puerto Rico from New York. He was outwardly genial and likable. I sold him a one-third interest in the investment company, and he also purchased one-third interest in a start-up electronics manufacturing company.

Sam checked out as an honest and well-meaning individual. But his open appearance belied a complex personality. Unbeknownst to me, he was an alcoholic. The other two investors were an attorney from San Francisco, whom I knew to be greedy and conniving, and his associate, who was kind of a 'good old boy'.

At this point, my investment company and my alcoholic associate owned one-third each; the attorney and his friend the other third. Since Sam was also a stakeholder in my investment company, I felt I could count on his vote to control the electronics company. I served as General Manager.

My previous business success made me feel infallible; that I could handle the crooked, greedy attorney. The initial business of winding miniature toroidal coils, followed by large orders for fractional horsepower motors from a leading aircraft manufacturer, resulted in rapid growth, and better than projected profits.

The following year, the attorney called a special Board of Directors Meeting and I found my genial associate, Sam, well lubricated with alcohol and no longer friendly. Clearly his vote would be with the other two owners and I would be a minority. Several proposals were made, all of which would drastically dilute my ownership, and negotiations continued for hours.

Finally, I agreed to sell my shares to the other investors for cash, based on the formula, "10 cents on a dollar," of the funds I had invested. My adversary was triumphant, almost gloating. He agreed to bring the final papers for signature in 2 days.

Enter the plan to make the Bad Guy Investors Finish Last. The Company badly needed new space. There was only one building available. The landlord, a friend of mine, agreed to make signing of the building lease contingent on my approval. The crooked attorney arrived with papers to sign. As I read them, he was confident, smirking at his victory over a difficult adversary. Wrong would triumph over right once again. I could read his thoughts.

"I did Russell in!"

I looked up from the documents.

"Everything is in order except for the amount of the check. It is only 10 percent of the original investment and we agreed upon *10 cents on a dollar or $1.10 for each invested dollar.*"

"Come on, Gardner, you're not that stupid. We'll just

dilute you out."

I returned the documents to him.

"Do whatever you have to do."

He was back the next day with a certified check for $1.10 per share, wide-eyed with new respect.

I said, "Should I ask for 20 cents on a dollar?"

But, I didn't. I remembered my father's counsel:

"Son, let your business adversary know that if you wanted to, you could 'spit in his eye'-- but never do it."

This was a lesson for me. I would never again become involved with a dishonest or greedy associate. Due to changing market conditions, the electronics factory closed less than a year later.

Illustration Capsule Three

Scenario: A good friend asked me to consult with him regarding his Florida investments, a roof truss manufacturing plant in Pensacola, and other ventures. I agreed.

One of the resident investors, who I replaced as Manager, was at his charming best. He said that I had been named by the Board of Directors to be President of the company which manufactured roof trusses. I promptly declined the honor in writing, because a president is *personally* liable for unpaid social security and income taxes, and delivered the letter to his office.

Rule: Never accept a position in a company, such as President or Executive Vice President, without knowing and weighing the risks. I entered the investor's office.

"We owe IRS $36,000 in unpaid withholding taxes and social security contributions. What do you intend to do?"

"Here is the check stub for full payment, made just last week," ("Yes, but I am not 'Johnny-off-the-pickle-boat'"), I thought..

When the offices closed Friday evening, I opened and read every file. There, in a file drawer tucked away in a folder, was the $36,000 check to the IRS, signature torn off. It had never been mailed. I made careful notes of all the files, finished the study early Sunday morning. Monday morning came.

"You were mistaken. Here is the check to the IRS."

He was unperturbed, as most rogues are when caught.

"My secretary made a mistake. I'll take care of it."

After we moved to Satellite Beach, Florida, an IRS field agent arrived at our home to collect the unpaid taxes, plus the fines, penalties, interest, etc. owed by the truss factory.

"Mr. Russell, we are informed that you are responsible for these unpaid taxes since you were President of the company when the debt was incurred."

My documentation was complete. I had never been President. The agent was very angry. "That man sent me on a wild goose chase. He will pay."

The Pensacola investor paid the debt over a period of years.

Here are two things to keep in mind:

1. *A title, such as President, Executive Vice President or even General Manager, may entail personal liability for unpaid Federal and state social levies and income tax withholding taxes.*

2. *When signing as an officer of a company, always include the title immediately after the signature to avoid personal liability.*

Illustration Capsule Four

Scenario: A large airfreight forwarding company was owned by two 50-50 shareholders. My client controlled sales and marketing, the other shareholder was responsible for finances and administration. The latter had skimmed at least $250,000 from the company, so there was little cash. An airline had to be paid $750,000 in 10 days.

"Gardner, you have to find me new investors to cover this payment or we are bankrupt!"

I did an in-depth review of the financial situation.

"Tom, there is no need to bring in investors, if you will agree to follow my recommendations."

We began an intensive collection effort and convinced major customers to make advance payments. At the same time, I was able to get major airlines to extend credit beyond the standard 10 days, but still had to devise a strategy to delay, for a few days, the large payment due.

I was relieved when a clerk -- not an officer -- called from the airline. I could hear sounds of a Christmas office party in the background. She asked if the check had been sent.

I replied, "We have been waiting for instructions as to where to send the payment, since our main offices have moved to Florida." I could tell she was anxious to rejoin the party.

"Please send the check to our Miami office, not to Tampa, because they would not know what to do with it."

That same day we mailed the check for the full $750,000... to the airlines' Tampa office. We were still short $100,000, which -- with a sigh of relief -- I collected 10 days later. As I had hoped, the Tampa manager held the check for 2 weeks awaiting main office instructions. The first critical hurdle had been overcome.

I strongly counselled the owner, "We have to move all corporate bank accounts from your state to Florida. There is too much money involved, and your associate has too many connections there."

He delayed. My concern mounted.

A telephone call to the bank confirmed my misgivings. "All Company accounts have been frozen by the court," the banker reported. The bank had also been named codefendant in the lawsuit filed by the adverse stockholder, who claimed my client was squandering the assets of the company. We had not been notified of the lawsuit because our own attorney had conspired with the other stakeholder, to have the funds impounded, then served *himself* as our company's registered agent.

Had I not called the bank, the funds in the company accounts would have been placed in court custody. The court clerk assured me that, once the funds were in the court jurisdiction, it would take 6 weeks -- at least -- to get them released. By that time the company would be insolvent. The banker obligingly faxed a copy of the lawsuit.

After studying the complaint for several hours, a strategy dawned. A clause in the complaint stated that frozen funds could be used only to pay legitimate accounts payable. I contacted the airline, which cooperated and provided us with a proper invoice.

The following day, Friday, our attorneys obtained a court order to instruct the bank to issue a cashier's check to the airline for the full amount frozen in the bank account -- $367,000.

We presented the court order an hour before bank closing

time, while the adversary shareholder and his (our) attorney were out of town. Bank officers scurried around frantically, and finally had no alternative but to issue a cashier's check, which we delivered to the airline that same day.

Crisis averted, the business prospered. It was not long before the bank balance averaged $1 million dollars. We fought off every legal attempt of the dissident shareholder, and ignored his threats. When I travelled to his city to negotiate the final settlement, my success at making another Bad Guy Investor Finish Last was highlighted when he asked,

"Aren't you afraid to meet with me, alone?"

How to Make a Bad Guy Lender Finish Last

Illustration Capsule One

Scenario: My client's high-rise building was now 80 percent complete. A REIT (Real Estate Investment Trust) from the East had been paying construction draws, but now was making excuses, demanding additional information, anything it seemed, to delay payment. My research indicated an alarming trend. Several projects financed by this REIT had been 'taken over', completed and sold out for the lender's benefit. Our project was obviously targeted for the same treatment. I also found that the principal owners came from a shady background, and were very tough. One of my investors told me that, when tempers heated up in a crucial meeting, the lender offered to, "Buy him a pair of concrete boots."

We also learned that one of the REIT's problem loans involved a failed gaudy motel called the *Roman Holiday* (each room had its own swimming pool) along the northern coast of Florida. It was suggested that our company purchase this 'dog motel' as we called it, to encourage the REIT to complete the funding of the high-rise building. Since the lender was under pressure from its investors -- because of the bad motel loan -- the concept was approved by them.

We insisted that our attorneys prepare the documents in such a way that, if necessary, we could impute the cost of the motel to our high-rise loan. This would make the loan usurious and the REIT would be in violation of Florida Law. The lenders' attorneys were aware of our intent, and twice amended the documents to thwart our defense. Our investors notified the lender that the changes were *unacceptable*. They finally decided to approve the original documents.

Payments again flowed, but the final 10 percent was withheld, even after final completion of the building. Our people brought an action against the REIT, alleging usury. The hearing before the judge lasted several hours.

Finally, His Honor said, "I am going to continue this case for 30 days. In the meantime," and he turned to look directly at the lender's co-owner, "I suggest you come to a settlement because, frankly, I don't know how I am going to rule."

In the resultant settlement, our investors' ownership was reaffirmed, and all 80 units were subsequently sold at a profit. The dog motel was returned to the lender. A year later, the co-owner of the REIT boarded an airplane on which I was travelling.

"Gardner, borrowers always try to claim usury, but you were the only one to make it stick. We were impressed. We have a problem for which we need your help. Are you interested."

Yes... I guess not!

How to Keep a Good Guy Investor from Being a Bad Guy

Illustration Capsule One

The time arrived for my Exit Plan to come true. The date to actually capitalize came about earlier than I had planned, because of two *unacceptable* -- to me -- business realities. First, I slept fitfully because I was co-signed on a substantial bank loan in Oklahoma. I discovered that my conservative nature did not handle that kind of exposure well.

The thrust of my four associates' argument was to use owner capital, with heavy emphasis on (necessary) debt financing. We shared equal ownership in *Borinquen Towers,* a huge high-rise project, a development of 1,000 homes, the *San Patricio Shopping Center,* and two tax-exempt factories.

One associate was a successful developer, another an attorney skilled in real estate law. The third was the owner of a huge mid-western chain of supermarkets, and the fourth, a young builder-developer who basically "ran the show."

I could have lived with anxiety-disrupted sleep, because of a multimillion dollar carrot, but not with the second reality. Every few months, the three U.S.-based investors came to the island of Puerto Rico. They loved to relax by the Caribe Hilton pool, then visit the casino late each evening. Around midnight we adjourned to one of the suites and began to negotiate the structuring of the 'next deal'.

A sumptuous midnight dinner, via room service, was followed by more discussions. About 3:00 a.m. -- and never earlier -- we gathered around the table to sign checks, pro-rata to our 20 percent ownership each. It came to me forcefully that I did not enjoy this ritual. So, I implemented my exit.

"I just realized that you four enjoy this," I said during a lull in the conversation. I immediately had their attention. "I don't. So, I want out."

There was at least a full minute of silence, then one investor said, "Gardner, if you can't afford to stay in, we will see you get your money back."

The Good Guy was about to become the Bad Guy investor.

I replied, "I can handle it fine, but I'd rather spend more time with my family. I talked with my attorney and asked him if he would buy my stock for (I named the attorney and the amount of his offer) and he assured me he would be delighted."

I knew that the three shareholders disliked that particular attorney. I continued, "But, since we are friends, I will offer my shares to you for somewhat less than his offer."

The deal was made. I was released from all bank and other obligations. And, like one of my early heroes, Rainsford -- the ultimate innovator in *The Most Dangerous Game* by Richard Connell -- said after his final life or death encounter, that, "(he) had never slept in a better bed..." I slept the night through without a care, and made a policy decision to never again personally guarantee any debt.

I recently read a book by a leading entrepreneur-author who related how he and his associates decided to sell a company with $100,000 of book value for $1 million. They 'convinced' a prospective buyer that they had a competitive offer, and got the price. There was no such offer. It was fictitious. The projections of the business obviously warranted the price tag, since it later out-performed the other companies in the buyer's portfolio. Some would call that "negotiating talk". My business life follows a different drummer because:

> *Premise: Any entrepreneur with a modicum of creativity will find ways to triumph through negotiation; to discern beforehand and thwart adverse plans of Bad Guys, or Good Guys who might become Bad Guys.*

*"Gelt" was a word first introduced into the Yiddish and German languages in the late 17th Century. It's principal meaning then, and now, is simply "money". During the past few decades *gelt* has also come to mean -- or so my Jewish business friends inform me -- money, jewelry and investments set aside and not to be touched except in the gravest of emergencies. It is in this context that it is used in this book, and in my own family tradition.

A poignant example is the possibly anecdotal account of refugee's shoes, hollowed-out heels concealing diamonds to ransom their lives if necessary.

CHAPTER EIGHT

THE GOLDEN FLEECE

An inescapable reality is that the most carefully prepared profit-and-loss and cash flow projections may prove to be less than reliable, because unforeseen changes in technology, customer acceptance, competition, and other factors, often militate to cause businesses to have a destiny of their own. As the Spanish say, *"El hombre propone y Dios dispone,"* (Man Proposes and God Disposes).

In both start-ups and acquisitions there are apparent and hidden contingencies and challenges; obstacles which make it more difficult for the entrepreneur to make dreams come true. And there is the ever-present danger of the *golden fleece.*

Recognizing and Preventing the Golden Fleece

The purchase of an existing company to add value in management expertise, new products and markets, is a viable alternative to the creation of a start-up venture. In *The Mid-Career Entrepreneur,* Enterprise Dearborn (1993), Joseph R. Mancuso outlines thoroughly how to successfully acquire a business. He has developed *The Search* almost into an art form.

There are usually more Buyers than there are Sellers. It is not uncommon for investor friends of mine to call me to see if I know of a business they might buy. My reply is nearly always, "Hey, if I knew of a good business for sale at a reasonable price, *I'd* buy it."

Unless deeply motivated, Sellers tend to overestimate their companies' value. If a Buyer has to look forward, after purchasing a company, to 8 or 10 years of profitable operations to recapture his or her investment, it is very unrewarding.

For favorable leverage and a payout in less than 5 years, look for troubled companies with inherent potential, but which suffer from lack of management, mismanagement, or financial anemia. Of course there must also be a motivated Seller.

And, though not for the fainthearted, there are companies in shambles, one step away from Federal Bankruptcy Court, which can be rescued through heroic effort.

Lastly, there are companies already under the protection of one or another of the federal bankruptcy laws, which might be attractive to a Buyer able to walk the company through the tedium of government regulations, in order to bring it to profitability, and out of bankruptcy.

The age and condition of the target company largely determine the number of challenges and contingencies which, unless identified and neutralized, might fleece the new owner of his or her investment.

At one extreme is the first type of entity noted above, probably overpriced, but with business affairs in good order. At the other extreme is the floundering, failing company, in various stages of disarray. The latter harbors not only contingencies, but costly surprises, intended or not, which require that the Buyer be vigilant to avoid the *golden fleece*.

Premise: The older the company, and the worse its condition, the more debris it accumulates, such as dis-

putes, pending litigation, labor claims, etc. In buying such a company or it's assets, allow a substantial 'fudge factor', a financial buffer for such contingencies.

Illustration Capsule One

I acquired a manufacturing company with a minimal positive net worth. Projections indicated that, by careful management, changes in product mix and aggressive marketing, it would become viable. The company had previously failed due to mismanagement. However, with the *law of the next optimist* at work, it was reorganized with new investors -- but with the same (mis)management -- whose investments had in turn been dissipated.

Due to the precarious situation of the firm, I structured the purchase of all the issued and outstanding stock on an option basis, so that I could cut my losses if unforeseen events prevented me from turning the company around. This was my fudge factor, my 'out' if everything turned to mud.

Dorothy, as my accountant, asked the President for the corporate books. He pointed to a box. There were records all right; three sets of books, each one a different bookkeeping system, which had been posted for a few months, then abandoned. I had personally taken a physical inventory, but had not personally verified the accounts receivable, which was a mistake.

I telephoned a customer, a friend of mine, who had been invoiced for custom mahogany desks.

"When can we expect payment?"

"What do you mean? The desks haven't been delivered yet."

I showed the invoice to the former CEO. He stood hipshot, squinting one eye against ubiquitous cigarette smoke as it curled upward. I asked if the desks were ready for delivery.

"No, they aren't manufactured yet." He continued,

"You see, in order to avoid a swing in sales from month to month, we *'pre-invoice'* in order to make the annual sales curve more uniform."

Now *that* was an original concept!

"Uh. How many other pre-invoices are there?"

The telephone interrupted our interesting conversation before he could reply. It was a vendor who wanted to know when his invoice would be paid.

"Dave, this invoice is not on the list of certified payables you gave me at closing," I said to the former CEO.

"Uh," again a thoughtful squint. "Guess I forgot it."

Every few days someone else called to request payment, with the same response, "Guess I forgot it."

A few months later, one of the former owners, a leading attorney, called to tell me that I owed more than 12 months unpaid rent on the factory building, and that it had to be paid or he would have to take legal action. Though I protested that this obligation was not included in our purchase agreement, he was adamant.

The situation called for firm, creative action. The facts:

1. There was no longer a positive but a *minus* net worth due to 'pre-invoicing' of several large orders -- which meant the *sale* had been recorded, but no costs against it; no materials, labor, or general and administrative expenses (G&A).

2. There were several thousand dollars of additional "Guess-I-forgot-it" accounts payable.

3. And, a former owner planned to take over the business by legal action unless I paid 'a year's back rent.'

I called my employees together and informed them that Mr. X, who owned the factory building, planned to try to take over the company, and that, as they knew, he had full-time guards watching the property to keep us from moving.

"If we're going to save the business, and your jobs, I'll need your help. I've rented space in a better location and installed wiring for the machinery and equipment. Tomorrow is Thanksgiving Day. Mr. X will be enjoying his turkey dinner and the guards will have the day off. I can't afford to pay you anything now to move the company. How many are willing to come early tomorrow morning?" They all raised their hands.

Shortly after dawn the following day, a big van quietly backed to the factory loading dock. By late morning, it was loaded and the building stripped, including wiring. We installed the machinery and equipment at the new location with quick-connect/disconnect plugs and were in operation the following Monday morning. The telephone rang.

"Gardner, what do you think you're doing?"

"We needed a better location for the factory. Didn't I tell you?"

"I have the same remedy, regardless of your move."

"That's right. Come and get the keys."

Silence. He knew it would cost many thousands of dollars to re-wire and install the factory at its old location.

I continued, "Though the unpaid rent you claim was not part of our deal, to show good faith, I am willing to give you 24 pro-rata postdated monthly checks -- no interest -- for the full amount."

I enjoyed seeing the cancelled check arrive with each monthly bank statement. The attempt to fleece had failed.

Months later, he called me.

"Gardner, you are the toughest businessman I know. Let's do a deal together."

Thanks -- but no thanks!

When I paid Mr. X for his shares of stock a little more than 2 years later, the negotiated amount was considerably less than the option formula, and included a deduction for *twice the back rent* he had forced me to pay.

He later said, almost plaintively, "You paid the others more for their stock."

"Because they had faith I would pay the corresponding option amount in full... and you didn't."

Illustration Capsule Two

Another acquisition was a manufacturing company of consumer products, which had sought protection from creditors by filing for Chapter 11 in Federal Bankruptcy Court. The Trustee approved our business plan, which included a modest investment. Due diligence followed, including verification of inventory, receivables, payables, etc. But, the cash flow was tighter than it should have been. Something had to be wrong.

As I once again reviewed the Operating Statements for the previous year, it seemed odd that a small profit had been realized on a lower volume of sales than the preceding year, in which the company had lost money. The light finally dawned. *Total sales had intentionally been entered twice; the costs only once.*

I asked the former owner, a genial rogue, how that had happened. He acknowledged that it 'must have been a mistake'. The accountant who prepared the statements was reputable, so I had not thought to question the Financial Statements. Especially since they had been prepared for submittal to a federal jurisdiction.

Premise: Never assume anything and double-check everything.

I could have sued the previous owner and his accountant, and most likely prevailed. However, my personal policy has always been to avoid -- and never initiate -- legal action, but be ready to defend against and win any action brought by others. It is far more profitable to devote energies to the project at hand than to litigate.

The question was whether to lose a relatively small investment and cut losses, or to go ahead with plans to build the company, in spite of its real minus net worth. I talked with our only competitor and he promised not to start a price war. Unfortunately, he did not keep his promise. In retrospect, it would have been more productive to walk away. But, for reasons not now recalled (one of them was probably wounded pride), the decision was made to continue.

The first priority was to improve quality and mechanize the plant to lower production costs. A design patent was granted for one of my inventions; a machine which performed seven of the eight production operations formerly accomplished by hand. Profitability increased and I finally sold the company for a modest profit. But, I learned that, *whatever can go wrong in a bankrupt company, will.*

Yet, I had avoided being fleeced.

Dangers of "Holding On"

An excellent guide which has served me well in my entrepreneurial life is taken from a passage of ancient scriptures. *"There is... a time to keep and a time to cast away."* (O.T. Ecl. 5:6). Yes, there *is* a time to hold onto and a time to sell a business. The ultimate decision should be governed by the potential 'shelf-life' and characteristics of the enterprise, and by the mission and purpose of the owner.

As for me, I have always taken the first profit and never looked back, content to count my gelt and move on to the next project. Let the new owners take the venture to new heights and reap the greater reward.

In their optimism, some owners plan to capitalize when the business peaks. That is a lot like trying to predict an upturn or downturn in the stock market. It is manifestly impossible. Others, through inertia or optimism, hold on until the company value has greatly diminished.

Premise: Implement the exit plan as soon as possible after planned parameters have been met. Don't let either optimism or greed keep it all from 'coming true'.

Example: Early this year, a designer and producer of consumer products asked me to advise him regarding a specific challenge. He shared an experience that took place 2 years ago, at what he now recognizes was the peak of his company's success. He refused a firm offer of high seven figures for 50 percent of his stock. Not long thereafter, unexpected and unforeseen changes beyond his control in economic conditions and the market, drastically curtailed the business, and the window of opportunity closed.

The False Promise of Net Worth

High net worth and book value tend to obscure a reality, which is expressed by a definition I once heard of a millionaire builder:

> *A millionaire builder is one who leases a new convertible, drives around with the top down with a new young blonde wife and her poodle, redecorates his apartment, and can raise $25,000 if his banker pushes him to the wall.*

Net worth does not necessarily equate to liquidity, nor does it contribute to gelt formation. Companies can and do choke for cash flow -- even fail -- even though their book value is substantial. Holding on too long may be detrimental to one's financial health.

You Never Have Anything Until You Sell Something

Like the above-described millionaire builder, and as previously noted, there are entrepreneurs who invest everything they have in the first venture, and incur a heavy load of debt. Total net profits after taxes are invested in new machinery, equipment, etc. As the enterprise grows, they and their families have little or nothing. Typically the home is heavily mortgaged. There is no gelt, no discretionary funds, and little or no flexibility. On paper, they may be multi-millionaires. But, they are living proof of the saying, "You never have anything until you sell something."

"But, why sell the stock or assets of that first venture, if it is profitable and shows every evidence that it will continue to be successful?"

That is a good question. My response is:

1. If the owner has a specific exit plan to sell that first venture upon reaching a certain net worth, profitability, or other measurement (unless there is an obvious windfall or bonanza), he or she should not be tempted to continue ownership in the company beyond that prescribed time.

2. A profitable business should be able to command a purchase price of three to five times the average annual earnings of the previous 3 years (a simple multiplier-type business valuation formula, which varies according to total book value and fixed assets). A small company with average earnings of $100,000 annually, can, all other things being equal, capitalize for $400,000 after taxes, a good enabling sum.

3. Most new enterprises have a specific life-span. The fact that 5 years is spoken of as the 'half-life' of a business is truer than some would like to acknowledge. And, companies that continue to be successful after 10 years are in the minority. Our filter factory is an exception -- no better product has yet been designed for the drip irrigation market.

4. Entrepreneurs tend to live in a state of anxiety until they 'sell something'. It is remarkable how much more sanguine they become after exiting the business with large amounts of capital in-hand. With it, the entrepreneur can satisfy nearly *all* worlds; create or purchase a new venture; set aside rainy day funds (gelt); provide a comfortable living and security for the family; and enjoy steady income from invested capital in preparation for the *retreading years*.

How to Sell a Company

A. *The Company with A Full Management Team.* A management team is a prerequisite to attract venture capital firms, which, if the owner is not averse to giving up 30 percent ownership or more, can help the company achieve second and third stage growth.

Likewise, many potential Buyers, individuals and companies, before considering an acquisition, require that an in-depth management team be in place. Using the example of a typical manufacturing operation, such an organization might include a President/CEO, Financial Vice President, Marketing Vice President, General Manager, Plant Manager, etc.

The transfer of ownership scarcely causes a blip in the progress of the business, because the stand-alone team will continue to operate without interruption under the new owners. This is the type of company which is most readily saleable because it requires no additional management.

B. *The Company Without a Management Team.* Many enterprises are basically sole proprietorships where the owner(s) manages the company, with one or two low to middle level employees. At most, there may be a General Manager and/or Sales Manager who work under the direction of the owner. Assuming that the owner wishes to capitalize and leave the company, the market for potential Buyers will, for the most part, be limited to several sources:

1. Those who have available and can contribute management resources to replace the former working owner of the company.
2. Competitors, who already have management in place, see this type of company as an ideal acquisition. They

already have a management team, and the acquisition will allow general and administrative burden to be spread across a greater volume of total sales. A side benefit is an upward nudge in profits as price pressure is reduced.

3.   Individual manager-investors who look to 'step into the shoes' of the exiting owner by acquiring the business and providing the necessary resources and management to take the business to the next stage.

In an entrepreneur's various ventures during his or her business life cycle, all of the exit plans noted above may be used -- and more. Example: My *exits* to date have been as follows:

- The common voting stock of the plastics manufacturing company was sold to a company on the NASDAQ stock exchange, with management in place.

- Assets of the filter-strainer business were purchased by the leading competitor.

- Common voting shares of stock in multiple manufacturing, housing and commercial development ventures were acquired by my associates.

- The electronics factory shares of common voting stock were transferred in an *involuntary* sale to co-owners in an exciting triumph over an intended golden fleece, for "10 cents on a dollar." (See Chapter 7.)

- A consumer products factory which was sold to the principal vendor.

How to Get the Best Price.

In the past few years, there has been an explosion in the number of companies providing business valuations. Part of this sudden growth is due to more frequent requests by the IRS for independent, third-party appraisals of decedents' estates.

Certified Public Accountants have discovered business valuation as a valuable adjunct to their business. Many CPA firms which offer this service have a Certified Valuation Analyst (CVA) on their staff.

To obtain the title of CVA, a candidate must complete a course of study offered by the National Association of Certified Valuation Analysts (for current lists of CVAs in each state, contact them at 1245 East Brickyard Road, Salt Lake City, Utah, or via the Internet at *http://www.nacva.com/index.htm.*).

Depending on complexity, business valuation of a small business might require 20 to 40 hours of the CVA's time, at rates that vary from $100 to $180 per hour. By applying different formulas and approaches, a CVA is often able to improve the net return to the Seller.

A few years ago, there were only two or three business valuation specialists in all of Florida. I personally studied all the applicable formulas and applied them to reach the highest justifiable selling price for our factory. Then I enlisted the services of a business valuation specialist to confirm my analysis. The third-party recommendation provided leverage to ultimately establish a higher selling price for the company's assets.

In most cases, when the time comes to implement the exit plan, it is advantageous toward the successful sale of a company or its assets, to have a recent business valuation at hand. It adds credibility and a climate of confidence, as do annual financial reports prepared by one of the major public accounting firms.

When there is evidence of serious interest in acquiring the company, it is vital to pre-qualify the potential Buyer. Ask about previous investments. Get banking and business references. Contact all possible sources. Order a personal credit check. There are many Internet credit services. My attorney recently 'pulled' a *fast-track* credit report used mainly for probate purposes, which was startling in its detail.

After doing the above due diligence, the Seller should be able to determine the following:

(a) Is the Buyer able and willing to perform? (Some are able, but unwilling, and vice versa).

(b) Does the Buyer have a history of *milking* an acquired company and letting it go back to the Seller. (It can be so unrewarding to receive a down payment, then find out it is the *only* payment one will ever receive, and then have to pick up the pieces of the company).

(c) Will the Buyer provide sufficient references and information for the Seller to make an informed judgment? If not, tell the Buyer that the only acceptable offer is "C.I.F". Should he or she ask what that means, smile and say, "Cash-in-Fist."

When negotiations begin, the Buyer may inquire as to the 'asking price'. Never divulge the desired price at this stage. A good answer might be:

"That depends on the terms. One amount would be acceptable as a cash offer, another for short-term, and still another for long-term. Which do you have in mind?"

This avoids a direct answer to the question, while suggesting that the owner might accept extended terms of payment, if necessary to obtain a higher selling price.

At the appropriate moment in the negotiations, bring out the most optimistic CVA business valuation, 'just as a point of reference'. Convince the Buyer to make an initial offer. If it is 'in the ball park,' agree to it in principle, then negotiate it upward. Use that wonderful word *'unacceptable'* when necessary to establish 'go-no-go' parameters in the negotiations (this term comes from 'go-no-go' gauges which precisely measure critical openings such as the gap in a spark plug, or distributor points on an automobile).

When the best offer is on the table, and there is basic agreement on the total purchase price, there are ways, through the use of 'add-ons', to increase the selling price by *as much as 10 percent.*

Example: "Are you interested in a non-compete agreement? (Most buyers are.) Do you prefer to include a non-compete clause in the Purchase Agreement, or in a separate side-letter agreement? Would a 5-year non-compete agreement be acceptable?"

Start with an amount of compensation (equal to 5 percent of the total selling price) as consideration not to compete with the company. Approval will usually be forthcoming. Then present the second add-on.

"We are still a little apart on the purchase price..." (pause) "As you know, I have a long-term loan outstanding from the company. Rather than deduct it from the selling price, would you be willing to carry it on the books until we work out a mutually acceptable way to handle it?"

The loan, which the owner should have had on the books

for at least a year prior to the sale, and been paying interest at an rate acceptable to IRS (today at 8 to 9 percent per annum) could be an amount equal to approximately 5 percent of the desired selling price. The Buyer is, after a period of time, to write the loan off. At that time, the Seller will be obligated to pay capital gains tax on the imputed income.

The Exhilaration of Redeeming "Sweat Equity"

There has been no greater 'high' in my business life than to realize, at closing of the Sale and Purchase Agreement, the tangible financial rewards of equity appreciation and recapture of deferred compensation. Prior financial sacrifices are forgotten. Every dollar of deferred fees has multiplied for my benefit. Yes! The fist of triumph is thrust to the sky.

There is a magic in this process which permits a mini-investment -- plus a lot of hard work -- to return 200, 500, 1,000 percent or even more on the original investment. Obviously, those able to experience such a high ROI are the creator-innovators who keep their day jobs, or have outside income to meet living expenses.

In the profitable sale of stock in various ventures as a co-owner -- where I provided basically full-time management and received an adequate salary and bonuses -- amounts paid to me pro-rata to my ownership interests brought a warm, fuzzy feeling of achievement. However, that feeling was never the spontaneous mental fist-pump of joy which came from closing on a sale of stock or assets, where an insignificant investment and unstinting sweat equity are rewarded. In such cases, it is as if something substantial has been created out of nearly nothing.

How to Begin Again

The individual who gives all of his or her assets and, directly or indirectly, offers substantial assets of family and friends upon the altar of The First Venture, truly 'goes for broke'. Unfortunately, should the first attempt fail, there could be nothing left with which to begin again. It might require 3, 5 or more years to pay off debt secured with personal signatures, pacify relatives and friends who suffered losses, generate a modicum of seed capital, and then organize a second enterprise.

Premise: One signature can and will place the signer behind the 'power curve' and dictate the course of his or her life for years.

Example: As an Advisor to several Boards of Directors and Boards of Trustees, I was asked last year to meet with each Division Manager, to review personal, business and financial situations and goals. One person had committed everything to a previous venture, as noted above. Though the manufactured product showed good innovation and creativity, the company foundered. The ongoing debt service taxed his salaried income.

He considered filing for protection under federal bankruptcy laws, but agreed to a plan to work with creditors, which brought greater proficiency to his work, and generated more personal income. Today he is free of back debt, and is rebuilding his asset base. But, nearly 4 years had elapsed in the process.

It is preferable to hold in reserve enough capital for a 'second try', in the event of a first failure. I vividly remember how Dorothy showed me that, even in the most dire financial situation, cash can be set aside. In the first stage of our initial venture, when meeting each weekly payroll was a real challenge, she told me that with our new baby, she needed a second automobile.

"Honey, you know our cash flow better than I. We just can't afford a second car."

She didn't say anything, which I interpreted (incorrectly) as assent. Not long thereafter, she announced she had a new (used) car.

"You see, I've been expensing some money every week for quite awhile," she announced.

I was momentarily speechless. But, that is how I learned that one can expense a small weekly amount in any business -- for a specific need -- even toward creating the second venture, should the first one blow out.

Whether the new enterprise is a start-up, or acquired from others, it is important that a limit be set on the investment. My own policy has been to invest up to $20,000 in stock and/ or loans in each venture (no increase allowed for inflation over 3 decades) with no personal signatures from myself or my wife, but with all necessary sweat equity.

Like most entrepreneurs, I do not knowingly take risks. After achieving our gelt and discretionary funds, it seemed almost unseemly never to have taken a risk, never to have reached for the gold ring. A suitable opportunity arose in a revolutionary (but unsuccessful) technique to recover micron gold. We invested $40,000 (which we designated as "throw-at-the-wall-money-to-see-what sticks") in a secondary recovery placer mine in the Four Corners area in Utah, along the Dolores River. The gold is still there.

Premise: Since there is no guarantee that the new enterprise will succeed, commit only a portion of available assets, in order to launch a second venture if necessary. A successful business is often the product of one or more previous failures.

Building Resources for the Retreading Years

Retirement programs, pensions, 401k plans, ESOPs, pensions, etc. are usually not part of the entrepreneur's lexicon. For several reasons, their business activity falls outside these 'safety nets'. First, is the lack of work continuity, since, on the average, they create and divest themselves of 5 different projects by age 55.

Second, though they receive Social Security benefits on basically the same level as the lifetime employee, it funds only one-third to one-half of the cost of living, and promises to be less in the future.

Most retirement plans are based on measurements of time/value such as a certain number of years of continuous employment, employee contributions to pension plans, vesting, insurance policies, etc. The creator-innovator, absent the option of traditional retirement plans, has no choice but to provide a comprehensive self-retirement plan toward a comfortable retirement, to avoid enforced *retreading* (i.e., the necessity to augment income by seeking work among limited employment opportunities available to senior citizens, or retraining for income-producing activities).

Rainy-day money is no longer sufficient. From the various ventures, some of which will have been successful, enough gelt must be set aside so that interest on the invested capital will defray ongoing living expenses. Today, if personal income of $50,000 a year is required, at least $1,000,000 must be working to produce it.

We pass along to the reader a simple financial plan which works for us. It calls for approximately one-third of total assets to be in income-producing residential revenue from single or duplex housing (with a goal to become mortgage-free by retirement age); another third in U.S. Treasury bills, which can be purchased direct from a Federal Reserve Bank, and/or time deposits in the form of FDIC secured instruments (Certificates of Deposit); and the remaining third in investments which we control. We have also opted to self-insure, except for modest insurance policies purchased years ago. If the reader notes the absence of stock market investments in the above, I can make no comment, since we have never had the talent to prosper in that arena.

Premise: By staying with a conservative, reduced-risk investment plan, the investor will inevitably be judged either unenlightened or brilliant, based solely on changes in economic conditions.

Example: Years ago the real estate market was booming. The manager of our local Citibank chided us for not investing, and for being too conservative -- the world and our business friends were passing us by. Then came a severe recession. The same bank manager congratulated us for being so astute, noting that 'cash was king', and I was one of the few able to benefit. He urged me to follow his example and liquidate all our assets. I thanked him and we kept doing what we had been -- and still are -- doing. It works.

The End.

FOR BELIEVERS

FOR BELIEVERS

To those of us who believe in some kind of divine guidance, eternal purpose, and ideal of service to Deity and fellowmen, the following is dedicated. Non-believers are invited to read these accounts; come to their own conclusions.

For us, business has always been -- first and foremost -- a vehicle, a means to provide the financial flexibility to enable us to serve in any capacity to which we are called by His Servants. Our total combined *full-time* voluntary religious service spans 20 years, one-fifth of a century, with all but one year in foreign countries.

A former U.S. Senator, who was my mentor in college, decried my decision to interrupt higher education to devote 34 months as a Mormon missionary in Argentina. "What a loss," he said, shaking his head. "When you return, your classmates will have all the good jobs and you will be left behind."

As I write this, our net worth is several times that of all but possibly one or two of my former classmates. We have never suffered by putting God and His Son first.

Illustration Capsule One -- Putting Him First

Our manufacturing enterprise was progressing, in spite of heavy pressure from a competitor. Asked to bid on a project, we were assured that the successful bidder would be awarded several million dollars in subsequent contracts. A formal bid opening was scheduled for a Monday at 2:00 p.m. The previous weekend had been devoted to religious conferences with a visiting authority of our church. Monday morning the telephone rang with a call from the authority, "Today, I would like to visit church members in outlying areas."

I did not have to consider. A decision had been made many years earlier to do anything the Lord asked. The Sales Manager was shocked to hear that he was to attend the bid opening in my place. We discussed strategy:

1. Our competitor's custom was to prepare two sealed bids, one higher than the other.

2. The value of the contract was, at a maximum, $150,000.

3. The competitor would expect us to offer something less than that. We considered $149,000. No, their owner, Mr. Y, would assume that's what we would do, and bid $148,000. Therefore, we would bid $147,500.

4. At 10 or 15 minutes before the bid's scheduled opening, Mr. Y (who did not know our Sales Manager) would see that I was not there. Figuring that no bid would be tendered by our company, he would register the higher of his two bids.

5. At 5 minutes before the bid opening, the Sales Manager would register our sealed bid.

Visits to church members were well-received and rewarding. At 2:20 p.m., I telephoned the Sales Manager.

"Mr. Russell, you must have a friend 'up there'. We won the bid by $137. Since our bid was so close and you weren't here, Mr. Y was convinced we paid-off their Vice President for Sales, and fired him."

Illustration Capsule Two -- The "Promise".

Assigned to a 3-year calling as Mission President for our church in Uruguay and Paraguay, we decided that, in order to maintain our standard of living and support two children in college, we would have to dip into our assets for tens of thousands of dollars.

It came to me, almost as a direct message, that whatever we spent during our assignment, would be returned to us, and that upon our return home, our Balance Sheet would be unchanged. I had no idea how this would happen.

Dorothy began to attend dealer auctions in Montevideo, Uruguay. She bid on 18-carat gold bracelets, chains, and gem-encrusted jewelry -- all at the market price for gold. When we had her collection appraised in Florida, 3 years later, gold prices had soared. The total appraised amount -- less payments to the auctioneer -- fully replenished our Balance Sheet, according to His promise.

We believe that, when we are in truly in the service of God and our fellowmen, we are entitled to guidance in our financial affairs and, at the very least, forced to be creative.

Only one of our friends improved his financial position during our absence. Others suffered losses. I told one former associate that, had he gone with us, he'd still be wealthy.

The reader, a Believer, will comprehend.

Illustration Capsule Three -- Replenishing

Over a decade ago, Dorothy was a real estate saleswoman, I was a management consultant. But, I was spending nearly full-time to raise the local members's 30 percent share of a million dollar "stake center" (which our faithful members along the Space Coast of Florida contributed in less than 6 months).

"How much do you think we earned together, last year?"

"I don't know. How much?"

She mentioned an amount in high 4 figures. We had been living on interest from our principal.

Sufficiently motivated, I "hit the ground running" and our cash flow improved.

One night I dreamt of seeing a sign that said, "Land Auction: Seaboard-something-or-other," (the lettering was not clear). In my dream I was told that we should get my friend, William Harrell, to go to the auction with us.

I told Dorothy of the dream. She said, "Why, there's a billboard on Post Road advertising the Seaboard Loan Company Auction. You must have seen it."

But, I had not been in that area for many months.

The auctioneer began to call for the bulk bid, a lump sum price for the entire 127 acres. We dropped out toward middle 6 figures. Then, as is the custom in such auctions, when the high bid is recorded, the total acreage was broken up into smaller parcels which were in turn put up for bid. This was done in the hope that the total combined bids for the individual parcels would bring more than the bulk bid. We were outbid on all but the last two parcels.

The next-to-last parcel of 27 acres came up. Someone made an opening bid. Dorothy bid 20 percent higher. The auctioneer became almost frantic trying to elicit a higher bid, without success. When he finally gavelled, "Sold!", so much time had elapsed that Dorothy wasn't sure it was still our bid.

The last parcel of 27 acres, identical to ours, went for enough to overtake the bulk bid. Three months later, our profit from the sale of the property -- *triple our investment* -- replenished our usual annual earnings.

In my mind, Providence had restored our missing income.

TRUTH

Truth is truth, wher'er 'tis found,
Whether picked up from the ground,
From the dust and dirt and grime,
Or in polished sands of time.

Truth is truth, wher'er 'tis seen,
Though as diamonds it may gleam,
And sparkle and scintillate,
Or lie in unpolished state.

Truth is truth, wher'er 'tis heard,
Whether flying as a bird,
Far above the clouds,
Or in grim spectres it enshrouds.

Truth, my friend, comes before you,
Soft spreads its mantle o'er you,
and bids you to expect it.
Will you accept or reject it?

Do you close your eyes and ears,
Does it cause you bitter tears,
When it changes your emotions,
And reverses former notions?

Great discoveries of the ages,
Unannounced by bards or sages,
Have verified Truth's position,
In spite of every opposition.

So this advice I give to you,
From whatever point of view,
When truth comes upon your vision,
Hold it not in derision.

For truth is truth in all ages,
Whether seen by fools or sages,
Prove all things, hold fast the good.
God would save you -- if He could.

Dr. Harry Hale Russell, LLD (grandfather) - 1921

BIBLIOGRAPHY

William Alarid	*Money Sources for Small Business* • Puma, 1991.
Rosabeth N. Canter	*The Change Masters* • Simon & Schuster, 1983.
Charles Coonradt	*The Game of Work* (Third Edition)
Clifford M. Baumbach & Joseph R. Mancuso	*Entrepreneurship and Venture Management Second Edition* • Prentice-Hall, 1987. (A 'must' for the prospective entrepreneur.)
David H. Bangs, Jr.	*The Start Up Guide, A One-Year Plan for Entrepreneur*s • Upstart Publishing, Dover, NH, 1989.
Robert Benfari, PhD	*Understanding Your Management Style* • Lexington Books, 1991. (A thorough analysis of personality measurement beyond MBTI.)
James C. Comiskey	*How to Start, Expand and Sell a Business* • Venture Perspectives Press, San Jose, CA 5th Printing 1989. (An excellent "How-To" publication.)
Peter F. Drucker	*Innovation and Entrepreneurship -- Practice and Principles* • Harper & Row, 1985. (Deep insight from the Master. The emphasis is on Internal Corporate Entrepreneurs.)
George Gilder	*Recapturing The Spirit of Enterprise -- Updated for the 1990s* • ICS Press, Institute for Contemporary Studies, San Francisco, CA, 1992.

Charles J. Givens	*Wealth Without Risk* • Simon & Schuster, 1988. (Valuable information for the entrepreneur.)
Arthur S. Grove	*High Output Management* • Random House, 1983.
Fred Klein	*Handbook on Building a Profitable Business* • Entrepreneurial Workshops Publications, Seattle 1990. (120 questions. Good insight.)
Joseph R. Mancuso	*How to Start, Finance and Manage Your Own Business* • Prentice-Hall, 1978.
	Fun & Guts • Addison-Wesley Publishing Company, 1973.
	The Center for Entrepreneurial Management, Inc. 83 Spring Street, New York City, NY 10012
	Mid-Career Entrepreneur • Enterprise - Dearborn, 1993.
Judith H. McQuown	*Use Your Own Corporation to Get Rich* • Pocket Books, 1991.
Ted Nicholas	*Secrets of Entrepreneurial Leadership* Dearborn Publishing, Inc., 1993. (Refreshing thoughts on entrepreneurial management methods -- with forms.)
Geoffrey N. Smith & Paul B. Brown	*Sweat Equity* • Simon & Schuster, 1986.
Linda Pinson	*The Home-Based Entrepreneur* • Out of Your Mind and into the Marketplace, 1989.

David Robinson   *What Is An Entrepreneur?* • Bob Adams,
                        Inc. Publishers, 1990.

Jeffry A. Timmons   *The Entrepreneurial Mind* • Brick House
                        Publishing Company, 1989. (Important
                        thoughts -- see Chapter 8, "What Skills Are
                        Needed for Excellent Self-Evaluation. Also
                        Chapter 12.)

Karl H. Vesper   *Frontiers of Entrepreneurship Research* •
                        Babson College.

APPENDIX A

Chapter I - *Understanding Your Management Style*
(The following has merit, but needs to be reviewed and
evaluated. I don't understand all of it.)

Additional Measurements for Management Style:
The MBTI, by Katherine and Isobel Briggs

Karl Jung's theory of classic Psychological Types is the
background for the MBTI tests for personality definition,
developed by Katherine Briggs and her daughter, Isobel, after
World War II.

According to Jung, everybody is either Extrovert (E) or
Introvert (I), and there are two rational or judgment functions,
thinking (T) and feeling (F), and two irrational or perception
functions, sensing (S) and intuition (N). There are four possible combinations of the four functions: sensation and thinking (ST); sensation and feeling (SF); intuition and thinking
(NT); and intuition and feeling (NT).

The extroverted types are: EST, ESF, ENT, ENF. The
introverted types are: IST, ISF, INT, INF. Thus, there are 8
types. The essence of the MBTI is that the Briggs have
identified 8 additional personality measurements types, for a
total of 16.

They added Perceiving (P) and Judging (J) to describe the
person who uses either sensing or intuition in these interac-
tions (P), or thinking or feeling in dealings with the outside
world (J) to help clarify which is the dominant personality trait
for each individual.

Thus the judging function (thinking or feeling) dominant
(J) becomes EST, ENT, ESFJ, ENFJ, INTJ, INFJ, ISTJ and

ISFJ. The perceiving function dominant (P) includes ENTP, ENFP, ESTP, ESFP, ISTP, INTP, ISFP and INFP.

ESTJ -- The Dominant Entrepreneur Personality

This extroverted type judges his environments through thinking, his dominant function; draws his conclusions from objective, external information. The external world is his reality and he demands that the rest of the world conform to his view of it. He interprets his environment through logic and careful organization. When a decision must be put on the table he readily supplies one. The ESTJ person readily grasps information, is apt to create new venues.

ENTJ

Like the ESTJ, he judges his environments through thinking, but vision -- and a sense of possibilities -- enter the picture. His dominant judgment function is based upon grasping the meaning of facts and things and their unique associations.

An ENTJ and an ESTJ might find mutual understanding in offering opinions, but would violently disagree as to whether their opinions were based on fact or fiction. The ENTJ is a natural 'commandant' who insists on ruling by his particular vision. In organizations, he is the one who looks to the future and conceives new ventures. If the tertiary sensing function is not brought into play, formulations may be nothing than pure fantasy. He is able to balance his vision with relevant facts.

APPENDIX B

Privacy and Asset Protection

It has often been said that it is easier to make money than to keep it. My clients have certainly found this premise to be true. There are in Nevada, and most recently, Alaska, provisions for privacy, asset maintenance, and protection, as well as some tax relief.

So-called Revocable Living Trusts offer relief from probate and death taxes, but provide no asset maintenance or protection, since thy are subject to creditor attack as if they were the individuals involved.

There are also Irrevocable Trusts and Private Foundations which are helpful in this regard. The latter are for the service-oriented, those who truly want to benefit humanity. By law 5% of the corpus must be distributed to tax-exempt 501(c)3 charitable entities annually. Good asset maintenance and protection.

In their desire for privacy, and concern about asset protection and tax relief, thousands of U.S. citizens are turning to offshore 'havens'. Before investing offshore, due diligence is important, as is the necessity that the entity created will pass the *Truth Test,* in the answer to the *Big Question.*

Imagine a deposition setting, which might take place after investing offshore. The IRS attorney asks the *Big Question.*

"Have you ever, directly or indirectly, caused or aided in the transfer of any funds or other assets whatsoever, be they your own or third-party funds and/or assets, outside the continental United States?"

Should the individual lie, and be caught, he or she may be charged with a felony. To avoid a lie, the response might be the unsatisfactory, "I don't remember," or , "I refuse to answer on the grounds that it might incriminate me.."

If the answer is in the affirmative, this next question will surely follow.

"Describe in what country and in what entities such funds are located."

It's a 'no-win' situation.

Premise: If the offshore investments require resorting to outright falsehood to accomplish their purposes, it not worth the game.

Some principals, I am told, deliver funds to their attorney who sets up the overseas investment. Then, they can truthfully answer, "No," to the Big Question. The attorney could then, presumably assert attorney-client privilege.

Some time ago I personally visited and evaluated major offshore jurisdictions which offer privacy, asset protection, and some tax advantages.

The privacy of overseas so-called 'havens', varies from 'somewhat' to very porous, due to mutual treaties between each jurisdiction and the U.S.

Some offer another level of asset protection.

Index

NOTES

Order Form

- Fax Orders: Advantage Publishing (407) 773-7085
- Telephone Orders: (407) 777-4548
- On-line Orders: russ@yourlink.net
- Mail Orders: P.O. Box 372358, Satellite Beach, Fl 32937

Please send ____copies of *THE EFFECTIVE ENTREPRENEUR* @ $14.95 each fob Satellite Beach, Florida 32937. (Discount Schedule to Apply)

I am including: (check one)
☐ $1.60 per book for U.S. Postal Book rate, or
☐ $3.20 per book for Priority Mail.

No other shipping or handling charge

Total amount of this order included $_____

I understand that I may return any books ordered from Advantage Publishing for a full refund; for any reason, no questions asked.

Company name:_____
Name:_____
Address:_____
City:_____ State:_____
Zip Code:_____
Telephone:_____Fax_____
E-Mail_____

Payment: Check or Money Order. For 30 days credit terms, (only if ordering multiple books) please provide credit references.

ADVANTAGE PUBLISHING
P.O. Box 372358
Satellite Beach, Florida 32937
407-777-4548 407-773-7085 Fax